Malta

WORLD BIBLIOGRAPHICAL SERIES

General Editors:
Robert L. Collison (Editor-in-chief)
Sheila R. Herstein
Louis J. Reith
Hans H. Wellisch

VOLUMES IN THE SERIES

VOLUME 64

Malta

John Richard Thackrah
Compiler

CLIO PRESS

OXFORD, ENGLAND · SANTA BARBARA, CALIFORNIA
DENVER, COLORADO

217477

016.9458
T 363

British Library Cataloguing in Publication Data

Thackrah, J.R.
Malta. – (World bibliographical series; v.64)
1. Malta – Bibliography
I. Title   II. Series
016.945'85   Z2375

ISBN 1–85109–007–X

Clio Press Ltd.,
55 St. Thomas' Street,
Oxford OX1 1JG, England.

ABC-Clio Information Services,
Riviera Campus, 2040 Alameda Padre Serra,
Santa Barbara, Ca. 93103, USA

Designed by Bernard Crossland
Typeset by Columns Design and Production Services, Reading, England
Printed and bound in Great Britain by
Billing and Sons Ltd., Worcester

THE WORLD BIBLIOGRAPHICAL SERIES

This series will eventually cover every country in the world, each in a separate volume comprising annotated entries on works dealing with its history, geography, economy and politics; and with its people, their culture, customs, religion and social organization. Attention will also be paid to current living conditions − housing, education, newspapers, clothing, etc. − that are all too often ignored in standard bibliographies; and to those particular aspects relevant to individual countries. Each volume seeks to achieve, by use of careful selectivity and critical assessment of the literature, an expression of the country and an appreciation of its nature and national aspirations, to guide the reader towards an understanding of its importance. The keynote of the series is to provide, in a uniform format, an interpretation of each country that will express its culture, its place in the world, and the qualities and background that make it unique.

SERIES EDITORS

Robert L. Collison (Editor-in-chief) is Professor Emeritus, Library and Information Studies, University of California, Los Angeles, and is currently the President of the Society of Indexers. Following the war, he served as Reference Librarian for the City of Westminster and later became Librarian to the BBC. During his fifty years as a professional librarian in England and the USA, he has written more than twenty works on bibliography, librarianship, indexing and related subjects.

Sheila R. Herstein is Reference Library Instruction Coordinator at the City College of the City University of New York. She has extensive bibliographic experience and has described her innovations in the field of bibliographic instruction in 'Team teaching and bibliographic instruction', *The Bookmark*, Autumn 1979. In addition, Doctor Herstein co-authored a basic annotated bibliography in history for Funk & Wagnalls *New encyclopedia*, and for several years reviewed books for *Library Journal*.

Louis J. Reith is librarian with the Franciscan Institute, St. Bonaventure University, New York. He received his PhD from Stanford University, California, and later studied at Eberhard-Karls-Universität, Tübingen. In addition to his activities as a librarian, Dr. Reith is a specialist on 16th century German history and the Reformation and has published many articles and papers in both German and English. He was also editor of the *American Society for Reformation Research Newsletter*.

Hans H. Wellisch is a Professor at the College of Library and Information Services, University of Maryland, and a member of the American Society of Indexers and the International Federation for Documentation. He is the author of numerous articles and several books on indexing and abstracting, and has also published *Indexing and abstracting: an international bibliography*. He also contributes frequently to *Journal of the American Society for Information Science, Library Quarterly*, and *The Indexer*.

Contents

Contents

Contents

Introduction

The Maltese archipelago, comprising the islands of Malta, Gozo and Comino and the tiny uninhabited islands of Cominotto and Filfla, is situated in the Mediterranean Sea, about 60 miles south of Sicily and 180 miles north of the African coast. Malta, the largest island in the group, has an area of a mere 95 square miles and the highest point of the island is only slightly over 800 feet above sea level. The island has no lakes or rivers and hardly any trees. Moreover, no mineral resources have been discovered there apart from salt. Notwithstanding this, historically, Malta has played a significant part in international affairs, because of its strategic importance and its fine natural harbours. Over the centuries, many nations have taken control of the islands in order to secure these advantages. Not suprisingly perhaps, the country's avowed aim today is to pursue a neutral foreign policy, and to create a viable economy, based not on the island's military value, but on tourism, industry and agriculture.

Little is known about the country until it was taken over by the Phoenicians in ca 800 BC. It was then colonized successively by the Greeks, Carthaginians, Romans and Saracens. In around 1090, Malta was occupied by the Normans of Sicily and this was the beginning of a period of great hardship for the islands. In the 15th century Malta suffered piratical raids and pestilence as well as a disastrous famine. In addition, in 1488, they endured the first concerted attack by the Turks.

In 1530, the year in which Emperor Charles V offered Malta to the Knights of St. John, the country was impoverished and desolate. However, since being expelled from Rhodes in 1522, the Knights had been searching unsuccessfully for a base in the Mediterranean and were therefore in no position to turn down the Emperor's offer. When the Knights arrived, few Maltese would have dared to hope for the protection and prosperity their rule would ultimately bring. The Order's early years were spent in fortifying the island, as they feared another assault by the Turks. Their apprehension was justified, as in 1565, the Turks launched an attack which became known as the Great Siege of Malta. Vastly outnumbered, the Knights nevertheless hung on to their positions and the Turks became increasingly demoralized as a result of heavy casualties, sickness and food shortages. Eventually the Turks were forced to leave the island and after the Battle of Lepanto (1571), which checked the Turks in the Mediterranean, a period of relative tranquility ensued.

The Knights made Malta into a bastion of Christendom, and developed it into a thriving trade and communications centre. After the Siege the Knights built a new town, with what it was hoped would be invulnerable fortifications. The town, which replaced Mdina as the capital of Malta, was called Valletta, after Jean de la Vallette, the Grand Master who had led the victory against the Turks in 1565. Successive grand masters continued the process of improving the island's defences and building new settlements, particularly around the Grand Harbour. The Knights' wealth brought prosperity to the island and their Christian values ensured that their rule was, by the standards of the day, fair and enlightened.

However, in the 18th century, there was a decline in the moral standards of the Order and the Knights became less monastic and more worldly. With this spiritual decline came financial weakness, when in 1792 their extensive possessions in France were confiscated. In 1798, Napoleon invaded Malta and without any resistance, the Knights departed. French rule was harsh and brutal, and accordingly in 1800 the Maltese rebelled and appealed to the British for help to oust the French. This was duly given, and two years later, the Maltese asked to be placed under British sovereignty. Under the 'Treaty of Paris' (1814), Britain formally annexed Malta.

Malta was extremely valuable to Britain because of its strategic importance. As a result the Maltese economy flourished throughout the 19th century, through the installation of military bases, the expansion of the shipbuilding industry and the improvement of harbour facilities. During this period, a succession of constitutions brought varying degrees of autonomy to Malta and the islanders constantly agitated for greater political freedom. In 1921, Malta was granted a constitution which gave the country considerable self-government, although Britain retained responsibility for the islands' foreign affairs. This constitution was suspended in 1930 and again in 1936, after further political crises, and in 1939, Crown Colony rule was reestablished.

During the Second World War, Malta played a crucial role in the Allies' Mediterranean strategy. The island was subjected to very heavy bombing and a naval blockade by Italy and Germany. Thousands of people were killed or wounded by air raids and starvation became an imminent possibility. As a recognition of the great courage which the Maltese had shown in withstanding the bombardment, King George VI awarded the George Cross to the whole island.

After the war, the desire for independence grew and throughout the 1950s, there were various proposals on the future status of Malta. In 1955, the integration of Malta with Britain was proposed at the Round Table Conference in London, but the idea received little support. Moreover, there was no consensus within Malta over the form that the future government of the island should take, and hence the negotiations with Britain proceeded slowly. Finally, in 1964, a draft constitution was prepared by the Maltese government and this was approved in a referendum held on the islands in that year. The British government agreed that Malta should become independent under this constitution and on 21 September 1964, Malta became an independent state and a full member of the British Commonwealth of Nations.

After independence, Malta was still used as a naval base by Great Britain, and when the Labour Party came to power in Malta in 1971, Prime Minister Dom Mintoff threatened to break ties with the West if Britain did not increase rental payments. After discussions, an agreement was reached whereby Britain and NATO would supply economic aid to Malta in return for the use of its naval base. This agreement was operative until 1979, when the last foreign service men left the island.

Since independence, Malta has officially been pursuing a policy of non-alignment, although some commentators believe foreign policy has been more Machiavellian than neutral. In 1984, this was even the opinion of Anthony Vassallo, Secretary General of the Community Party of Malta, which normally supports the Labour Party's foreign policy. Mintoff, however, argued that if his country was to survive the closing of the naval base, he would have to seek new allies and gain assistance from wherever possible. In 1972 Malta signed a cultural agreement with Libya, and throughout the 1970s, the country has had increasing military and trade links with the Soviet Union. Indeed, in 1981, the Soviets gained the use of the former NATO oil bunker operations, although they rescinded the agreement in 1983. In addition, however, China, Abu Dhabi and Saudi Arabia have also supplied financial aid to Malta. It has been Malta's friendship with Libya, however, that has been particularly controversial and the Libyan connection has certainly been a significant factor in Malta's attempts to gain industrial investment and make good the loss of British aid.

After 1964, relations between Britain and Malta became increasingly strained. Britain criticized what it believed to be Mintoff's heavy-handed approach toward political freedom and education and was suspicious of his foreign policy. In return, Mintoff banned British journalists from the island and closed down the Malta radio station of the British Forces Broadcasting Service, which he claimed produced biased reports. Despite this political friction, British holiday-makers remain vital to the Maltese economy. In 1981, for example, 705,710 tourists visited Malta, of whom 514,062 were British. In the summer, Malta averages over ten hours of sunshine each day, there are good beaches and the island is suitable for water sports, such as boating, scuba diving and water skiing. Together with its attractive scenery, and the growing interest in the island's archaeological sites, there is every sign that Malta will retain its popularity as a holiday resort.

Politically, Malta's future is uncertain. In December 1984, Dom Mintoff resigned as prime minister and the policies of his successor, Carmello Mifsud Bonnici are still largely a matter of speculation. Some commentators believe he will adopt a more rigidly left-wing stance than Mintoff, whose policy of 'positive neutralism' enabled him to ally Malta with any nation that would be useful. One of Bonnici's problems will certainly be with the Roman Catholic Church. There has been unresolved friction between the Church and the Labour Party since the 1960s, principally over the Labour Party's belief that the power of the Church should be substantially reduced. This long-running dispute does not help to endear the party to the electorate, in a country where over 90% of the population are practising Catholics.

Whether the country moves further left under Bonnici, or whether the right-wing Nationalist Party is returned to power in the 1986 election, Malta's important position between east and west will ensure continued interest in the fortunes of this small island.

Introduction

The bibliography

This bibliography, although it does not claim to be comprehensive, does pay attention to almost all aspects of Maltese life, past and present. Considerable effort has been made to ensure that a balance is maintained between older works of enduring value and newly published material. A wide variety of social and political views are represented and the general aim is to stimulate the reader to consult the works described in this bibliography. In keeping with the format of the series, almost all the works mentioned are in English. This has necessitated some restriction in the coverage, particularly of recent works, as since independence most of the books published in Malta have been in the Maltese language.

Some entries are relevant to more than one category, and when this is the case, the item has been placed under the heading deemed most appropriate to the central theme of the book or article described. The bibliography is aimed primarily at the English speaking reader who has a serious interest in the country and its culture, but who is not a specialist. Any errors which may have crept in are entirely the author's responsibility and the reader has my apologies.

Acknowledgements

I am grateful to all those who have helped me in the compilation of this book, particularly, the former librarian of Rhodes House, Oxford, F. E. Leese; the current librarian of Rhodes House Dr. A. S. Bell and the assistant librarian Mr. A.M. Lodge; Donald Simpson of the Royal Commonwealth Society, London; Miss E. C. Blayney of the Foreign and Commonwealth Library; Mrs. Patricia A. Larby of the Institute of Commonwealth Studies, London; Stanley Gillam of London Library; Dr. G. M. Bayliss of the Imperial War Museum; Dr. V. A. Depasquale of the Malta Library in Valetta; Dr. Paul Xuereb of the University of Malta Library at Msida, Malta; Francis S. Mallia of the Museum Department in Valletta; Mr. P. J. Camilleri of the Malta Government Tourist Office in London; and Luke Trainor, editor of the Commonwealth and Colonial History Newsletter of the University of Canterbury, New Zealand.

Lastly, my grateful thanks both to Dr. Robert Neville and Sarah Stubbings of Clio Press, Oxford, for their encouragement, help and advice and also to my typist.

John Richard Thackrah
August 1985

Theses and Dissertations on Malta

A. J. Baldachino. 'Financial institutions in Malta 1800-1975', BLitt thesis, University of Oxford, 1976. 209p.

B. W. Beeley. 'The individual and changing rural society in Malta: a study of some aspects of the social and economic geography of the Maltese islands', PhD thesis, University of Durham, 1960. vol. I. 423p, vol. II. 65p.

J. F. Boissevain. 'Maltese village politics', PhD thesis, University of London, 1962. 281p.

Joseph D. Bugeja. 'British influence on Maltese development 1919-1933', BLitt thesis, Oxford University, 1973. 225p.

S. Busuttil. 'The economic development of Malta 1946-1962', PhD thesis, University of Manchester, 1963. 626p.

W. A. Charlton. 'Trends in the economic geography of Malta since 1800', PhD thesis, University of Durham, 1960. 250p.

Francis Chetcuti. 'Modernising educational administration to facilitate the formulation and implementation of plans, with special reference to Malta', PhD thesis, University of London. 1971. 283p.

J. A. J. Debono. 'The contribution of the Catholic Church to the development of a system of popular education in Malta with special reference to primary and secondary schools during the British era 1800-1964', MPhil thesis, University of London, 1975. 753p.

J. A. J. Debono. 'The language problem and educational policy in Malta 1800-1975', PhD thesis, University of London, 1982. 771p.

Emanuel P. Delia. 'The interrelationship between emigration and economic activity in Malta', DPhil thesis, University of Oxford, 1980. 471p.

Geoffrey H. Dench. 'The London Maltese: collective responsibility and community structure', PhD thesis, University of London, 1972. 321p.

J. M. Enriquez. 'Achievement, motivation and entrepreneurial occupation in Malta', MSc thesis, University of Bristol, 1970. 159p.

E. L. Galea. 'Education in the Maltese islands 1800-1966', MPhil thesis, University of Southampton, 1969. 699p.

Henry J. Frendo. 'The formation of Maltese political parties 1880-1926', DPhil thesis, University of Oxford, 1976. 291p.

A. M. Hoppen. 'The fortification of Malta by the Order of the Hospital of St. John of Jerusalem 1530-1798, with special reference to Valletta and Floriana', PhD thesis, University of St. Andrews, 1970. 543p.

J. McLeman. 'A demographic study of St. Paul's parish, Valletta 1595-1798 using the method of family reconstitution', PhD thesis, University of Aberdeen, 1979. Vol. I 523p. Vol. II 342p.

R. G. Milne. 'Contribution of public expenditures to social development: a case study of Malta 1945-1967', MPhil thesis, University of London, 1973. 295p.

Miles K. Oglethorpe. 'Aspects of economic evolution of Malta since independence in 1964', PhD thesis, University of Glasgow, 1983. 448p.

M. Pirotta. 'The British services sector in Malta 1946-1979', BA thesis, University of Malta, 1977. 136p.

Charles Archibald Price. 'Maltese emigration 1826-1885: an analysis and a survey', DPhil thesis, Oxford University, 1951. 634p.

M. Richardson. 'Aspects of the demography of modern Malta: a study of human geography of the Maltese islands', PhD thesis, University of Durham, 1960. 280p.

A. Rushton. 'The physical and agricultural geography of the Maltese islands', MSc thesis, University of London, 1948. 172p.

M. Vassallo. 'Religion and social change in Malta', DPhil thesis, University of Oxford, 1976. 388p.

Edward Lawrence Zammit. 'Maltese perceptions of power, work and class structure with special reference to the drydocks' shop stewards', DPhil thesis, Oxford University, 1979. 427p. 56p appendixes.

Edward Lawrence Zammit. 'The behaviour patterns of Maltese migrants in London with reference to Maltese social institutions', BLitt thesis, Oxford University, 1970. 367p.

The Country and Its People

1 **Why Malta? Why Ghawdex?**
Dunstan G. Bellanti.   Hamrun, Malta: St. Joseph's Institute, 1934.
128p. bibliog.
A study of the origins of the names of the Maltese islands and their towns and
villages, together with an examination of the early history of each parish.
Ghawdex is the Maltese name for Gozo.

2 **Malta, a companion to the landscape.**
B.W. Blouet.   Valletta: Progress Press, 1963. 136p. bibliog.
The opening chapters of this illustrated volume outline the island's history. Blouet
then goes on to describe a series of excursions around Malta, which set the towns,
fortifications and countryside in their historical background.

3 **The story of Malta.**
B.W. Blouet.   Valletta: Progress Press, 1981. 239p. 21 maps and
figures. bibliog.
A general historical and geographical survey of Malta, from prehistory to the 20th
century. It does not put forward any new theories but is nevertheless an ideal
introduction to the splendour of the islands. Three appendixes list Malta's grand
masters, civil commissioners, and Governors-General and prime ministers.

4 **Hal-Farrug: a village in Malta.**
Jeremy Boissevain.   London: Holt, Rinehart & Winston, 1969.
128p. map. bibliog. (Case Studies in Cultural Anthropology).
This case study in cultural anthropology examines the richness and complexity of
life in Hal-Farrug. The work emphasizes the importance of the Catholic Church
and analyses social integration and political rivalry.

The Country and Its People

5 **Maltese memories 'Tifkiriet'.**
  Eric Brockman. London: Allen & Unwin, 1944. 134p. map.
This work represents an appreciation of the love and friendship that was extended to the author by the Maltese people. A faint image of the true Malta, which is so different from the remarkable island of popular myth, and which the author believed was near its end, can be glimpsed in these pages.

6 **Last bastion, sketches of the Maltese islands.**
  Eric Brockman. London: Darton, Longman & Todd, 1961. 253p.
  bibliog.
A collection of disparate writings which provides a composite picture of the islands. The book contains much heartfelt appreciation of the Maltese people and the topics covered include: the author's first impressions of the islands; leisure; the Knights of St. John; race and language; 'festa-1926'; and songs. A very informative appendix on Maltese spelling is also provided.

7 **Malta and Gozo.**
  Robin Bryans. London: Faber & Faber, 1966. 256p. 2 maps.
A personal and rather romantic view of the islands which refers, for example, to the waterfront bars and tiny cafés, to the bird catchers, to the flower-covered fields in winter, to the sun, warm sea and to beaches, coves and bathing. Special attention is paid to the influence of religion in the islands. Since the time when St. Paul was ship-wrecked on Malta religion has, for many islanders, been an extremely important aspect of life. Today religious processions are much in evidence and there is, of course, widespread belief in the saints and in holy visions.

8 **Malta's Covent Garden: the Valletta Market.**
  A. Crossthwait. *Country Life* (1982), p. 434-35.
A very interesting account of the remarkable diversity of the Valletta Market covering its historical, social and economic development.

9 **An essay on Malta.**
  Nigel Dennis, with drawings by Osbert Lancaster. London: John Murray, 1972. 54p. map.
This work is sympathetic to the aims of the National Trust of Malta which has made great efforts to preserve the landscape and historical buildings of Malta and Gozo. Eleven beautiful illustrations supplement the text. The aim is not to provide a tourist guide, but to convey to the reader Malta's special qualities including: its history; the language and character of the people; the styles of architecture; and the particular nature of the rural landscape.

10 **Fact sheets on the Commonwealth: Malta.**
  London: Central Office of Information, 1966. 7p. map.
This interesting but now somewhat outdated pamphlet, aimed primarily at the businessman, covers geography, population, government, history, the economy, and social welfare.

11 **Crossroad isle: people of Malta.**
Gerald Formosa. Vancouver, Canada: Skorba Publishers, 1980.
93p.
Of the many books on Malta now available few have focussed photographically
on the people, their ordinary lives and daily activities. This book of photographs
fills this gap and is a personal observation of everyday life in Malta.

12 **Malta an island republic.**
Eric Gerada-Azzopardi, with photographs by Christian
Zuber. Boulogne, France: Editions Delroisse, 1980. 269p. map.
bibliog.
A general appreciation of the island, containing some superb colour photographs.
Malta's geographical location and magnificent natural harbours have meant that
the islands have played an important role in the history of the Mediterranean.
They have often been invaded and subjected to various rulers. The country's
passionate adherence to Catholicism is perhaps the only stable element of its long
history. It is no longer a foreign military base (the British forces left on 31 March
1979), and the economy now relies on industrial growth. In this new role, Malta is
attempting to promote an image of peace and friendship with all its neighbours.

13 **Malta: a survey, 1966.**
M. C. Hewitt. Oxford, England: 1966. 41p. map.
A useful, comprehensive concise politico-economic survey, which covers
geography, demography, agriculture and employment.

14 **Living in Malta or Gozo.**
Philip Hickson. Valletta: Agius & Agius, 1970. 68p.
This booklet, based on the author's experiences, aims to assist the new resident
during the first few months after his or her arrival from Britain. Useful chapters
include those dealing with the move from Great Britain to Malta; settling in;
accommodation planning; heating in winter; the retiree; living in Gozo; clothes
and storage; and some problems associated with Britain, including taxation
reports.

15 **The brass dolphins.**
Christopher Kininmonth. London: Secker & Warburg, 1957. 244p.
map.
An illustrated description of the Maltese archipelago with a strong historical bias.

16 **Malta: isles of the middle sea.**
Walter Kümmerly. London: George Harrap, 1965. 107p.
This work discusses Maltese archaeology, history, politics, society, language,
folklore and art, and stresses the importance of tradition in the islands. Illustrated
with colour plates.

17 **Malta's heritage: selections from the writings of E. R. Leopardi.** Valletta: Progress Press, 1969. 136p.

A collection of short articles, which first appeared in *The Times of Malta*. Each of them covers a different aspect of Maltese life, reflecting the author's wide-ranging interests. The articles are arranged under the following headings: 'Early fragments'; 'The notable city'; 'The knightly imprint'; and 'Of things Maltese'.

18 **Golden Malta.**
Hubertus von Mackensen, translated by David Ward. Msida, Valletta: Audio Visual Centre, 1981. 132p. bibliog.

This work, which contains a commentary in English, French and Maltese, is principally a collection of photographs depicting what the author considers to be the 'ideal' Malta.

19 **Malta.**
London: HM Stationery Office, 1964. 30p. 2 maps. bibliog. appendix.

An official publication outlining the strategic importance of Malta, its commitment to Catholicism, and its uniqueness as a colony, which also provides a brief political and economic history of the last 100 years in Malta. The work highlights the fact that, by the middle of the 20th century, Malta was less important to Britain as a military base, as capital ships were not being used so much. The appendix contains the constitution of Malta at the time of independence in 1964, along with an account of the referendum held in Malta in 1964 and the proposed agreement between Great Britain and Malta on finance and mutual defence and assistance.

20 **Malta a diplomatic press survey.**
Diplomatic Bulletin no. 24 (Dec. 1954), 44p. map.

This special edition is a patriotic and descriptive account of: reconstruction after the Second World War; industry and commerce; agriculture and fishing; education and culture; and health and social services in Malta.

21 **Malta G. C.**
London: British Society for International Understanding, 1952. 24p. (British Survey Popular Series, no. 81).

An illustrated description of Maltese life in the early 1950s which covers religion, the importance of emigration, and the spectre of unemployment. Includes an aerial view of Malta which shows the devastating effect on the island of German bombing during the Second World War.

22 **Malta handbook.**
Valletta: Information Division, Maltese Government, 1985. 172p.

An official publication, based on data submitted by Malta's ministries and government departments. It provides information of a general nature about economic and social conditions on the islands and cultural affairs and also refers to the tourist industry. The handbook also describes how Malta is governed and outlines the responsibilities of individual government departments.

23 **Malta Who's Who.**
Valletta: Progress Press, 1964- .
Since 1968 this volume has been published once every two years but initially this
was an annual publication.

24 **The Mediterranean.**
Jasper More. London: Batsford, 1956. 336p. 2 maps.
An introduction to the region as a whole, covering its history, character and
present-day circumstances is followed by a survey of the individual countries. A
large proportion of the brief section on Malta (p. 167-75) deals with the Knights
of St. John. The work contains many photographs.

25 **Malta: a handbook to the island.**
Sean O'Callaghan. London: Palmerston Press, 1968. 79p.
A concise but very comprehensive work on Malta's attractions, amenities, its
people, history and climate. It also pays attention to the island's industry.

26 **The Maltese islands.**
Charles Owen. Newton Abbot, England: David & Charles, 1969.
190p. 4 maps. bibliog.
An illustrated account of the islands' history and geography written for the
layman, with appendixes on Maltese rulers and important historical events,
principal feast days, a climatic table, and the Maltese alphabet.

27 **Face values: some anthropological themes.**
Edited by Anne Sutherland. London: British Broadcasting
Corporaton, 1978. 287p.
This book was written to accompany the series *Face Values*, first broadcast on
BBC 1 television in April 1978. It was a joint project between the BBC and the
Royal Anthropological Institute to explore the nature and meaning of human
differences. Chaper 5 (p. 108-37), by Jeremy Boissevain covers the Maltese
islands and it demonstrates how the traditional view of the sexes has survived and
is supported by the Maltese Civil Code. Women stay at home with their children
while the men have an active public role. The class system is strong and divisive,
although religion helps to unite the opposing groups and the church has a central
role in the community. Religion and politics are closely linked in Malta and
during the late 1950s and early 1960s, the church vigorously supported the
conservative Nationalist Party. Independence and the stream of tourists have
given the Maltese a new self-consciousness and a more developed sense of
patriotism. Parish patriotism or parochialism is also very strong.

28 **Contributions to Mediterranean studies.**
Edited by Mario Vassallo. Msida, Valletta: Malta University
Press, 1977. 283p.
A collection of papers presented at a symposium on Mediterranean studies held in
Malta. The first section provides a general account of Mediterranean history,
including a paper on the Maltese economy in the Roman period. The second

section deals with aspects of Iberian history, and the third discusses Maltese life and history, and includes two papers in Italian. The themes of section three are: clergy concubinage; the development of medicine and surgery; the plagues of 1675 and 1813 in contemporary poetry; changes in the epidemiologial pattern of disease; religious symbolism in a changing island; the changing status of women; and contemporary Maltese literature and theatre.

29   **A Maltese boyhood: interpolations.**
    Philip Ward.   Cambridge, England: Oleander Press, 1976. 49p.
A brief, highly personalized account of the author's early years in Malta. His poetic and at times mysterious style is an attempt to reproduce the thoughts of his boyhood.

30   **Camera, pictures of Malta.**
    F. Weston, M. Weston.   Valletta: Progress Press. 84p.
A collection of black-and-white photographs, which captures the beauty of the islands.

31   **Intimate Malta.**
    George Zammit.   Valletta: Midsea Books, 1978. 62p.
The country which is presented in these sketches is very different to the one advertised by the travel agents. It is the Malta that the inhabitants appreciate and love. The author has endeavoured to capture that elusive quality which gives the island its individuality.

Geography and Geology

32 **Malta our island home: a first geography of Malta.**
B. Leo Barrington.   London: Macmillan, 1970. 84p. map.
This introductory geographical work was written to foster a knowledge of Malta among the youth of the country. The author emphasizes the danger of ignorance in a democracy.

33 **The islets of Comino and Filfla.**
Charles J. Boffa.   Hamrun, Malta: Lux Press, 1966. 38p.
This booklet provides a description of the two islands, their landscape, coastline, geological formation and historical associations.

34 **The Mediterranean lands.**
J. J. Branigan, R. Jarrett.   London: Macdonald & Evans, 1975.
628p. (New Certificate Geography Series, Advanced Level).
The opening chapters of this textbook provide a geographical account of the Mediterranean area as a whole. There is also a useful chapter on p. 349-56 entitled 'The Maltese islands' which covers the structure and relief of the islands, climate and vegetation, history and people and the economy.

35 **Malta: a geographical monograph.**
M. W. Bruce.   Valletta: Progress Press, 1965. 75p. 10 maps.
bibliog.
This illustrated geographical survey commences with the theory that in pre-Pleistocene times, there was a land bridge from Sicily to the north African coast and that present day Malta is the shrinking surface of that previously much greater land area. It goes on to discuss Malta's landscape, most of which is cultivated because of the country's remarkably high density of population (the highest of any European country, at 3,075 people per square mile). Finally, Bruce

considers the essential duality of the Maltese economy, which was then based on both agriculture and on the value of the harbour to other countries.

36 Malta: an anthropogeographical study.

L. H. Dudley Buxton. *Geographical Review* vol. 14, no. 1 (1924), p. 75-87. map.

The great density of the Maltese population supported on a rock where the soil seldom exceeds a few inches in depth is a major anthropogeographical puzzle. The problem is raised in this article which analyses the history of man on the island. It covers: changes in population type; occupation by an Armenoid people; cultural connections with Carthage and Rome; Arabic influence under the Knights and the later history of the island. It also contains estimates and censuses of the Maltese population.

37 Sixteenth century Maltese cartography.

A. Ganado. *Sunday Times of Malta* 29 December, 1974.

The Siege of Malta in 1565 created a need for more detailed maps, as a successful defence of the island depended in part on a knowledge of the terrain. This article discusses the development of cartography which took place as a result of the siege.

38 The geology of the Maltese islands, with special reference to water supply and the possibilities of oil.

Herbert P. T. Hyde. Valletta: Government Printing Press, 1955. 135p. bibliog.

This booklet aims to present the geological phenomena of Malta in such a way that it will be understandable to the non-specialist.

39 Report on the geology of the Maltese islands including chapters on possible ground watertables and prospecting for mineral-oil and natural-gas.

Valletta: Government Printing Press, 1932. 37p.

This geological survey arose from the compilation of a report on sewerage and the saving of water in Malta.

40 An historical geography of Malta.

Frederick B. Singleton. M.A. thesis, University of Leeds, 1950. 38p. 4 maps. bibliog.

The main aim of this thesis is to assess the influence which geographical factors have had on Malta's history. Singleton makes a distinction between historical events which were influenced by the island's geography, and those which were not affected by it. The period of British rule is examined in detail, because at that time there were many issues which showed the link between history and geography. The author claims that Malta has had a significance out of all proportion to its size, the number of its inhabitants or its material resources. Appendixes cover population and trade statistics.

41   **Quaternary conditions in Malta.**

C. T. Trechmann.   *Geological Magazine*, vol. 75, no. 883 (1938), p. 1-26.

A description of the geologically 'sinking' island of Malta, with special reference to pebbles of limestone in Quaternary beds, problems of land bridges, fissures and Quaternary sections.

Travellers' Accounts

42 **Sir Walter Scott in Malta 21 November-13 December 1831.**
    Carmelo Mifsud Bonnici. *Malta Government Gazette*, 1932. 4p. 3
    appendixes.
A speech made on 21 September 1932, by the Minister for the Treasury, Carmelo
Mifsud Bonnici, on the occasion of the unveiling of a tablet to commemorate
Scott's visit to Malta.

43 **A tour through Sicily and Malta in a series of letters to William**
    Beckford of Suffolk from P. Brydone.
    Paris: J. G. A. Stoupe, 1780. 2 vols.
Written for the amusement of his friends and as an aid to his memory, this is an
account of the author's immediate impressions of the islands. It is one of the first
records of this kind to be published.

44 **Poetry into public servant.**
    Kathleen Coburn. *Transactions of the Royal Society of Canada*,
    Third Series. vol. 54 (1960), p. 1-11.
A brief survey of Coleridge's visit to Malta in 1804.

45 **A voyage in vain. Coleridge's journey to Malta in 1804.**
    Alethea Hayter. London: Faber & Faber, 1973. 182p. bibliog.
Material from Samuel Taylor Coleridge's notebooks and letters has been used to
compile this illustrated account of the poet's visit to Malta. It is divided into two
parts entitled 'Beckoning hope' and 'Vanishing hope', which document
Coleridge's disappointment in not finding the 'good life' which he sought in
Malta.

46 **Malta: an account and an appreciation.**
Sir Harry Luke. London: Harrap, 1960. 2nd rev. enlarged ed.
260p. 2 maps.

The author was in Malta during a very turbulent period of its history, and much of this account is based on his experiences during this time. The volume also includes an interesting chapter, which records the following people's views of Malta: Patrick Brydone, Lady Hester Stanhope, Coleridge, Byron, Disraeli, Sir Walter Scott, Thackeray, Edward Lear, Rudyard Kipling and D. H. Lawrence.

47 **Edward Lear, the life of a wanderer.**
Vivien Noakes. London: Collins, 1968. 359p. bibliog.

A fascinating, illustrated biography of Edward Lear, including his visit to Malta, in April 1866, which he described as being dreadful.

48 **Samuel Taylor Coleridge in Malta and Italy.**
Donald Sultana. New York: Barnes & Noble; Oxford, England: Blackwell, 1969. 429p. 3 maps. bibliog.

In 1894 Dykes Campbell announced in his biography of Coleridge that the archives connected with his public secretariatship in Malta had been burnt. Since then, it has been assumed that little can be known about this important period of Coleridge's life. However, this work has brought new material to light. Sultana claims that Coleridge's poor health, together with his addiction to opium, were responsible for his failure in Malta, both as a public secretary and as a writer.

49 **Benjamin Disraeli in Spain, Malta and Albania 1830-32, a monograph.**
Donald Sultana. London: Tamesis Books, 1976. 78p. bibliog.

An account of a journey which exercised a decisive influence upon Disraeli's personal and literary development as well as affecting his foreign policy when he became Prime Minister. While in Malta, Disraeli was particularly interested in the immunity enjoyed by Roman Catholic priests from the secular courts, which was something the British government had long considered an anomaly.

50 **The Siege of Malta rediscovered: An account of Sir Walter Scott's Mediterranean journey and his last novel.**
Donald E. Sultana. Edinburgh, Scotland: Scottish Academy Press, 1977. 215p. bibliog. 4 maps.

A study of Scott's Mediterranean journey and his last novel 'The Siege of Malta', which he wrote during it. This novel, although it was the central literary feature of Scott's last journey, had gone comparatively unnoticed by his biographers, until the appearance of this volume by Sultana, because the manuscript itself has not only remained unpublished, but is virtually unknown. This account outlines Scott's last journey and connects it with his novel of Malta, which he conceived at Portsmouth, started in Malta and completed at Naples. It then goes on to describe the manuscript, with special reference to its alleged incompleteness and to the existing pagination, which is peculiar.

11

51 **New approaches to Coleridge: biographical and critical essays.**
Edited by Donald Sultana.   London: Vision Press; Totowa, New
Jersey: Barnes & Noble, 1981. 246p.

Donald Sultana's essay 'Coleridge's political papers in Malta', (p. 212-241) is the
part of this wide-ranging volume which is relevant to Malta.

52 **The importance of Malta considered in the years 1796 and 1798, also
remarks which occurred during a journey from England to India,
through Egypt in the year 1779.**
Mark Wood.   London: John Stockdale, 1803. 78p. map.

A travel account assessing the commercial and political advantages which Britain
could gain from taking possession of Malta.

Travel Guides and Tourism

53 **Gozo.**
Brian Blouet.   Valletta: Progress Press, 1965. 60p. bibliog.
An outline history of Gozo is followed by a short description of the island's tourist attractions — its beautiful countryside, the Castello and its Rabat, the coastline and the little villages. This volume also covers the tiny islands of Comino and Cominotto. Another useful volume by Blouet is *The story of Malta* (q.v.)

54 **Malta: a history and guide.**
Brian Blouet.   Valletta: Progress Press, 1966. 118p.
Part one of this volume outlines the island's history and part two is a guide to its towns, countryside and fortifications, which are set against their historical background. The chapter on Valletta is a useful guide for the visitor who has only a few hours to spend in the capital. Great emphasis is placed on the influence which the Knights of Malta have had on the development of the island.

55 **Tourism and development in Malta.**
Jeremy Boissevain.   *Development and Change*, vol. 8, no. 4 (1977), p. 523-38.
Argues that tourism in Malta between 1964 and 1976, caused pollution, overcrowding and the destruction of important traditional values.

56 **A to Z of Malta and Gozo. Street and foothpath guide of the Maltese islands.**
J. G. Borg.   Marsa, Malta; Interprint, 1977. 167p.
This collection of maps indicates bus routes, footpaths, and interesting places to see on the islands.

57 **Gozo tourists' attractions.**
Michael (Lino) Caruana. Floriana, Malta: Empire Press, 1972. 32p.
This work, by a young Maltese journalist, provides details concerning places of interest to the tourist.

58 **The Mosta Rotunda, short history and guide.**
Raymond Cauchi. Mosta, Malta: Cauchi's Emporium, 1976. 78p.
This is the first short, accurate guide in English to the Rotunda, and fills a long felt need. It concentrates on a description of the church rather than its history.

59 **Malta.**
Edited by Thornton Cox. New York: Hippocrene Books, 1982.
120p. (Thornton Cox's Travellers' Guides Series).
There have been several editions of this concise guide to the islands which provides practical advice and information for the visitor. The volume covers Malta, Gozo and Comino.

60 **Malta.**
Edited by Peter McGregor Eadie. London: Ernest Benn; Chicago,
New York, San Francisco: Rand McNally, 1979. 128p. 2 maps.
(Blue Guide Series).
A sophisticated travel guide, illustrated with photographs and plans, which include ten suggested tourist routes. Since the late 1960s, the Maltese have tried, successfully, to expand the tourist industry and annual arrivals of tourists increased from 138,000 in 1968 to 425,000 in 1978. In 1981, tourist arrivals numbered 705,710, 514,062 of whom were British. It should be noted that Malta has more hours of sunshine than any other country in Europe, and that tourism is now of vital importance to the Maltese economy.

61 **Walks in Gozo.**
H. H. Hick. Valletta: Progress Press, 1953. 107p.
An illustrated photographic description of eighteen walks, with a summary and glossary describing the beauty of Gozo. It is based on the ordnance survey map of the island. All the walks start and finish at Rabat, the island's capital.

62 **Malta: blue-water island.**
Garry Hogg. London: Allen & Unwin, 1967. 248p.
A personal view of Malta is presented in this volume. The inclusion of anecdotes, snatches of conversation and vignettes make an important contribution to its appeal. It is illustrated with copies of oil paintings and photographs of the islands and will appeal to both serious readers and those who are content to turn an idle page.

63 **Malta and Gozo.**
Christopher Kininmonth.   London: Cape, 1970. 216p. 14 maps.
(Travellers' Guides Series).

The author's love of the places and people of Malta is evident in this photographic account. The book covers, for example, the prehistoric sites and the baroque buildings of the Knights of Malta.

64 **Walks and drives on ancient Gozo.**
Harrison Lewis. Gerrards Cross, England: Colin Smythe, 1974. 32p. map.

This illustrated guide, detailing twenty-five walks and drives on Gozo is a companion volume to *A guide to remote paths and lanes of ancient Malta* (1974). It is designed to introduce the visitor to the island's beauty spots and its rich architectural heritage. The exact direction of each route is indicated on a map, and differentiation is made between those suitable for walking and driving.

65 **Malta.**
Lausanne, Switzerland: Berlitz, 1982. 128p. maps. (Berlitz Travel Guide Series, English edition).

A factual, easy to read and up-to-date guide. It provides a brief introduction to the country, an outline of its history and a summary of the interesting places to see on the islands, including a useful chapter on Malta's archaeological sites, which are now an important tourist attraction. A variety of activities are covered, such as sports, shopping, dining out, festivals and nightlife. Colour photographs and maps, plus a special 'Practical information' section, covering such matters as health and medical care, transport and accommodation, add to the value of this concise volume.

66 **Malta: the island of sunshine and history.**
Valletta: Government Printing Press, 1947. 35p.

An interesting brief guide based on a number of sepia photographs.

67 **Malta: the jewel of the Mediterranean.**
Valletta: Government Printing Press, 1980. 144p.

This illustrated volume designed for tourists presents Malta as a land of romance, sunshine and colour.

68 **Tourist guide to Malta and Gozo.**
John Manduca.   Valletta: Progress Press, 1973. 127p. 5 maps. bibliog.

A compact, illustrated guide which will help the tourist to make the most of his stay on the islands.

69 **Tourist guide to city of Mdina.**
    John Manduca.   Valletta: Progress Press, 1975. 66p. 5 maps and
    plans. bibliog.

Mdina is one of the few remaining mediaeval and Renaissance fortified cities in
Europe. Its atmosphere and its buildings, including Spanish and Siculo-Norman
palaces and churches are unique. Inhabited since prehistoric times, and the
island's capital until 1568 when the Order of St. John built Valletta, Mdina has a
long and chequered history.

70 **Tourist guide to harbours of Malta.**
    John Manduca.   Valletta: Progress Press, 1976. 37p. bibliog.

There is a great deal to interest the tourist in the forts, churches and palaces of
the Grand Harbour and Marsamxett Harbour areas. This lucid guide, with its fine
black-and-white photographs is an ideal introduction to the harbours of Malta.

71 **Your Guide to Malta G.C.**
    Nina Nelson.   London: Alvin Redman, 1969. 221p. 5 maps.

A deep and close look at some of the interesting tourist attractions of Malta. The
guide is written with the package holidaymaker in mind.

72 **Malta.**
    Nina Nelson.   London: Batsford, 1978. 160p. 6 maps.

An illustrated, enthusiastic and well-informed guide to the island, combining
information and anecdotes about life on the island. Details of local handicrafts
and cuisine are also included and the work contains above average photographs
and sketch maps.

73 **Exploring Gozo.**
    Roger Parnis.   Valletta: Progress Press, 1966. 63p. bibliog.

A descriptive and leisurely account of eighteen walks on Gozo with useful tips.
Especially helpful are the seven appendixes relating to: English equivalents of
Maltese words; how to get to Gozo; hotels in Gozo; the Museum Department;
religious orders; and a summary of places to visit.

74 **Exploring Malta.**
    Roger Parnis.   Hamrun, Malta: Lux Press, 1973. 54p.

Many of the walks described have been designed for those without a car, and in
most cases they touch bus routes at several points. To cater for both car owners
and bus users the walks include circular itineraries and cross-country excursions.
The author indicates the places where the walker can leave a particular itinerary
and cut over to another route if necessary. He also states how much time is
required to complete the walks but the times stated should be regarded as the
minimum required for a fast walker.

75   **Illustrated guide to historic Malta.**
F. R. G. Pearce.   Valletta: Giov. Muscat, 1967. 198p. 2 maps.

Malta is an island of stirring panoramas, brilliant moonlit nights and enchanting sunsets and, as the author indicates, there are 'a hundred-and-one more things to excite the visitor's curiosity'. This volume is of value to the sightseer interested in novelties and curiosities and directs the reader to the island's prehistoric temples, catacombs, grottoes, palaces and churches. It contains numerous photographs and plans.

76   **The Xaghra monumental church.**
Julian Refalo Rapa.   Victoria, Gozo: Orphan's Press, 1969. 113p.

Based on ancient documents, this is a guide to the author's native village church, paying particular attention to the works of art which are to be found there.

77   **Your guide to Malta.**
Harold Rose.   London: Alvin Redman, 1963. 238p. 6 maps. bibliog.

This well researched guide, the result of a number of visits, clearly demonstrates the author's enthusiasm for the islands. Part one offers a general description; part two deals with the coastal area; part three with the interior; and part four covers Gozo and Comino. The volume also contains detailed appendixes.

78   **Malta and Gozo.**
Hermione Ruth Sacks.   London: New English Library, 1976. 124p. bibliog.

A comprehensive guidebook, covering a wide range of topics from sporting activities to ancient monuments. It also provides a brief overview of Maltese history, culture and archaeology, and includes a glossary of archaeological terms.

79   **The Palace of the Grand Masters: now residence of the Governor of Malta and its art treasures.**
Edward Sammut.   Valletta: Progress Press, 1960. 61p.

A detailed, well-illustrated guide to the palace. Two appendixes list the grand masters, governors and civil commissioners of Malta.

80   **The monuments of Malta – the ancient capital city of Malta and its art treasures.**
Edward Sammut.   Valletta: Progress Press, 1967. 46p. map.

An illustrated guide to the fortifications, the cathedral, the cathedral museum, Norman House, St. Paul's Square and the Carmelite Church. Appendixes itemise grand masters and bishops since 1530.

81   **Valletta: A guide to the capital of Malta GC and her art treasures.**
Edward Sammut.   Valletta: Progress Press, 1968. 64p. map.

A general history of Valletta is followed by suggested tours of the capital, which take in Grand Harbour, St. John's Cathedral and museum and the Grand Master's Palace.

82 **See Malta and Gozo.**
Inge Severin. London: Format Books, 1979. 144p. 10 maps.
bibliog.

A complete guide with itineraries, maps and a gazetteer, which covers Malta's
history, archaeology, art and architecture, flora and fauna.

83 **All about Gozo old and new.**
Edited by Antoine Vassallo. Victoria, Gozo: A. Vassallo, 1981.
96p. map.

Historical and cultural details as well as tourist information are contained in this
volume which is an ideal souvenir or gift for emigrants and prospective visitors.

84 **Walks in Malta – an archaeological and historical guide.**
F. Weston. Malta: *Daily Malta Chronicle*, 1931. 204p.

A description of the interesting sights in Malta, which includes details of twenty
routes for walks on the island. A great deal of attention is paid to festas and
customs of the island.

85 **A practical guide to Malta.**
R. J. L. Wilkinson. Valletta: ABC, 1950. 132p. bibliog.

The author aims to provide information for intending residents, holiday makers
and others who wish to increase their knowledge of this fascinating country. This
was the first major guide to Malta to be published after the Second World War,
and although dated is still of interest.

86 **The travellers' guide to Malta and Gozo.**
R. J. L. Wilkinson. Valletta: ABC, 1975. 120p. map.

A fully illustrated travelogue, which also contains a short history of the island.
The text is in English, French and German.

87 **Malta-Mellieha-the Riviera.**
Loreto Zammit. Valletta: Progress Press, 1958. 45p.

The natural beauty and archaeological wealth of Mellieha make it a very popular
resort. This guide to the peninsula is particularly useful for its historical and
topographical descriptions.

88 **Wied iż-Żurrieq and its beauties.**
Loreto Zammit. Valletta: Government Printing Press, 1965. 16p.

A comprehensively illustrated account of the Wied and nearby Blue Grotto,
which are two of Malta's beauty spots in the south-west of the island.

Flora and Fauna

89 **Birds of the Maltese archipelago.**
David A. Bannerman, Joseph A. Vella-Gaffiero.   Valletta:
Government Printing Press, 1976. 550p. bibliog.

This is the first comprehensive and illustrated description of the hundreds of different species of birds recorded in the Maltese islands, and it is also intended to serve as a general handbook on central Mediterranean ornithology. It documents the important role of the archipelago in bird migration between Europe and Africa. The authors provide a great deal of new information, based on their varied field experiences. The names of the species are given in the scientific trinomial form, and in English, Maltese and Italian.

90 **The ichthyology of Malta.**
G. Despott.   Valletta: Critien's Press, 1919. 59p.

A systematic list of 272 Maltese fishes, highlighting the great variety of species and the possible development of a Maltese fisheries industry. Before industrial potential can be assessed, investigations are needed in connection with the spawning habits and migrations of fish.

91 **Common beetles of the Maltese islands.**
A. Caruana Gatto.   Valletta: Giov. Muscat, 1894. 14p.

A guide for the layman written in a popular style. The work is elementary and deals with species in a superficial way. It was compiled to rectify the dearth of information about Maltese coleoptera.

92 **Buskett and its natural history.**
S. M. Haslam, assisted by P. Y. Royle.   Msida, Valletta: Malta
University Press, 1968. 52p. map.

This volume deals with various methods of investigating the outstanding natural history of Buskett, which is the most fertile area of Malta. It is useful for teachers as it includes suitable essay questions and exercises for school students. Soils, geology, climate, plant and animal life and human intervention are all covered.

93 **A flora of the Maltese islands.**
S. M. Haslam, P. D. Sell, P. A. Wolseley with contributions by J.
Borg, H. Micallef, M. Rix.   Msida, Valletta: Malta University
Press, 1977. 560p. map. bibliog.

A comprehensive guide to the flora of the Maltese islands, illustrated with one species of each genus. An excellent glossary is provided.

94 **A revised check-list of Maltese algae.**
Edwin Lanfranco.   Sliema, Malta: National Press, 1969. 24p.
bibliog.

This work provides a preliminary list of 296 species of algae and is designed for people coming to Malta to carry out research in marine biology, including research on algae.

95 **The natural history of Malta as presented by Abela in 1647.**
Guido G. Lanfranco.   Valletta: the author, 1955. 62p.

The Maltese historian Gian Francesco Abela, made many references to geology, botany and zoology in his work, and these are discussed in this study by Lanfranco.

96 **A complete guide to the fishes of Malta.**
Guido G. Lanfranco.   Valletta: Department of Information and
Tourist Services, 1965. 95p.

Malta is an ideal station for the study of marine life as shown by this guide book for beginners which contains over 260 illustrations of fishes. Only the most important Latin names have been included and the work is lavishly illustrated.

97 **Field guide to the wild flowers of Malta.**
Guido G. Lanfranco.   Valletta: Progress Press, 1969. 151p.

A comprehensive account with over 600 illustrations. Its aim is to help people on field studies to identify specimens of flowers.

98 **Guide to the flora of Malta.**
Guido G. Lanfranco.   Valletta: Progress Press, 1955. 99p.

This book, which is suitable for a person embarking on a study of botany, is particularly valuable for establishing plant names. A beginner is unable to make significant headway with Latin names and morphological terms, without the aid of diagrams, and the illustrations in this book are thus extremely useful. The work contains many common species and some rare ones, but some common plants have been excluded as the author restricts the coverage of the work to 300 species.

99 The Maltese dog.
Virginia Leitch.   Riverdale, Maryland: Jon Vir Kennels, 1953. 458p.

The primary purpose of this illustrated study was to collect in one volume the views of hundreds of writers on the subject of the Maltese dog. The work describes its origin and development in various countries, dog clubs, dogs in art and products made from dog combings.

100 How to raise and train a Maltese.
Arthur Liebers.   Jersey City, New Jersey: T.F.H. Publications, 1962. 64p.

A book written to cater for the increasing popularity of the Maltese dog in the USA. The 3,000-year history of the fluffy white Maltese testifies to its popularity through the ages, particularly as a pet for women and children. Despite their delicate appearance, Maltese dogs are healthy and long-lived as long as they are well cared for. The volume covers history, selection, care, housebreaking, obedience training, caring for females and raising puppies, and showing the Maltese.

101 A revised check-list of the birds of the Maltese islands.
C. de Lucca.   London: E. W. Classey, 1969. 95p.

This work provides a systematic listing of the genera of birds on the islands. It presents a comprehensive picture of the present status of each species, which will be of value to both the specialist and the amateur ornithologist.

102 The birds of Malta.
B. L. Roberts.   Valletta: Progress Press, 1964. 168p. bibliog.

This book fills a long-felt need, for until now the literature of the bird-life of the Maltese islands has been extremely scanty and has been confined mainly to a few scientific papers and inadequate lists, not all of which were reliable and many of which were inaccessible. This survey of Maltese ornithology brings together the work of disparate authorities, field notes, the experiences of bird watchers and the author's own experiences. It deals with 319 species, 125 of which can be seen fairly regularly during the year. English, scientific and, where applicable, Maltese names are given throughout. Black-and-white drawings and an index of scientific names make this work very appealing for both the specialist and the amateur ornithologist.

Flora and Fauna

103 **Bird studies on Filfla.**
Joe Sultana, Charles Gauci.   Valletta: Ornithological
Society,1970. 32p. bibliog.

The information in this comprehensively illustrated volume was gathered from a number of ornithological journals. Its aim is to interest the general public in the birds of the islands and to encourage concern for their protection. The authors hope to arouse general interest in birds among the Maltese and thus safeguard their future. The findings are based on studies made during five expeditions.

104 **A new guide to the birds of Malta.**
Joe Sultana, Charles Gauci.   Valletta: Ornithological Society,
1982. 207p.

Considerable attention has been placed in this volume on the natural history of a growing number of surviving birds in Malta. More reserves are now being built but trapping and shooting continue. This new guide provides information on the birds that breed in Malta and on the behaviour of various migrants during their presence on the island. It is not intended to serve as an identification guide.

105 **The butterflies of the Maltese islands.**
Anthony Valletta.   Malta: the author, 1971. 64p. bibliog.

A work in four chapters with lavish black-and-white illustrations describing in detail the lepidoptera of the islands.

106 **Look at Buskett.**
S. M. Haslam, assisted by P. Y. Royle.   Valletta: Department of
Education, 1967. 78p.

A teacher's guide which includes a nature trail, a glossary of plant names and a quiz.

107 **The moths of the Maltese islands.**
Anthony Valletta.   Faringdon, Oxfordshire, England: E. W.
Classey, 1974. 118p.

This volume aims to bring together all the records of moths that were made in Malta and Gozo between 1858 and 1972. It is a valuable contribution to the study of Maltese lepidoptera, as the last comprehensive list was compiled by Professor Borg in 1932. Valletta himself, along with the late Dr. Delucca, has recorded over 240 species in the last 38 years. These, together with the species recorded by other experts, are all included in this volume.

Prehistory, Archaeology and Ethnography

108   **The Hal-Saflieni Hypogeum, Paola, Malta – guide book.**
A. J. Agius.   Rabat, Malta: Palbo Printing Press, 1975. 32p.
bibliog.

This short volume provides a guide to, and description of, the Hal-Saflieni Hypogeum, a magnificent complex dating back to ca.2400 BC. The discoveries of a graffito showing the imprint of a hand and a bull schematically painted in black pigment are particularly interesting. A chart of the Neolithic, Bronze and Copper ages is included.

109   **Punic rock-tombs near Pawla, Malta.**
J. G. Baldacchino.   *Papers of the British School at Rome*, vol. 19 (New Series, vol. 6), 1951. 22p.

The discovery of rock tombs in Malta is not a rare occurrence, but in the majority of cases they are found opened and rifled of all material. The Punic rock tombs are thus particularly interesting, in that, when opened, almost all of them were still intact and relatively well preserved.

110   **Malta and the Mediterranean race.**
R. N. Bradley.   London; Leipzig, Germany: T. Fisher Unwin, 1912. 336p. map.

The author examines the characteristics of the pre-Aryans in Europe and traces the migration of Eurafrican and Mediterranean races to Malta. Considerable attention is paid to Malta's prehistoric monuments and to their relationship with those of the Eurafrican peoples.

111 The centuries look down.
Hugh Braun.   London: Richards Press, 1947. 256p. 2 maps.
Based on a survey undertaken during the Second World War, this is a very personal view of Malta's archaeology.

112 Sicily before the Greeks.
L. Bernabo Brea, translated by C. M. Preston, L. Guido.   London: Thames & Hudson, 1957. 206p. 7 maps. bibliog.
Richly illustrated with seventy-eight photographs and fifty line drawings, this volume surveys the Palaeolothic, Mesolithic, Neolithic, Copper and Bronze ages and discusses their interrelationship in terms of archaeological finds in the Mediterranean. Practical information on the sites is included at the end of the work. The study is relevant to Malta because the archaeology and ancient history of both Sicily and Malta are very similar. In particular, Malta's Tarxien temples closely resemble the temples in Sicily.

113 Seeking the site of St. Paul's shipwreck.
W. Burridge.   Valletta: Progress Press, 1952. 51p. 4 maps.
A description of the author's visit in 1948, to the site of St. Paul's shipwreck on Malta.

114 Further great stones, Gozo, explored in 1893.
A. A. Caruana.   *Archaeological Journal* (June 1896), p. 140-43. 2 plates.
This article analyses the results of an archaeological survey of the great stones Tal-Qaghan, Ta-Mrezbiet, Hagra Wieqfa and Hagra at Sansun.

115 The meaning of the Maltese countryside.
Paul Cassar.   Valletta: Progress Press, 1960. 72p. bibliog.
This booklet outlines the characteristics of the Maltese countryside, and shows why it developed as it did. It traces the origins and history of the following aspects of the landscape: rocks and stones, caves, cart ruts, pottery sherds, ancient tombs and catacombs, stone age temples, land cultivation, fruit trees, windmills, towers and forts and inlets and bays.

116 Signs of the gods?
Erich von Däniken, translated from the German by Michael Heron.   London: Souvenir Press, 1980. 224p. bibliog.
Chapter three of this volume, entitled 'Paradise of unsolved puzzles' (p. 82-136) relates to Malta. It considers the puzzling existence of 'ruts' in the stony ground of the islands and provides possible explanations for their presence. Von Däniken also studies the possible origin of the gigantic monoliths, such as the monolithic temple of Hagar Qim and the Hal-Saflieni prehistoric hypogeum. It is a very thought-provoking study, which leaves both the reader and the author with many unanswered questions.

117 **The Phoenico-Graeco-Roman Temple and the origin and development of Fort St. Angelo.**
J. F. Darmanin. Valletta: Progress Press, 1948. 131p. bibliog.

This illustrated monograph of the St. Angelo Fort is mainly intended for the student of Maltese history but it will also be of some interest to the more general reader. It is compiled from the Archives of the Order of St. John and the manuscripts in the Royal Malta Library, and takes into account the conflicting views of various historians.

118 **The prehistoric antiquities of the Maltese islands: a survey.**
John Davies Evans. London: Athlone Press, 1971. 260p. bibliog.

This volume provides details of the twenty-four archaeological sites in Malta, and the six in Gozo, including a list of the materials which were discovered there. It is extensively illustrated with plans, figures and plates. Except for certain sherds of special importance, only complete or substantially restored pots are listed here. The bibliography aims to be as comprehensive as possible in listing references to Maltese prehistoric antiquities before the year 1900. However, it is more selective in its coverage of post-1900 publications, omitting casual references and secondhand reports or evaluations. It includes Bronze Age settlements, 'cart tracks', finds of unknown provenance in the National Museum, cultures and chronology, and catalogues of the sites. Three indexes cover sites, geographical and personal names and there is also a general index.

119 **The megalithic monuments of Malta.**
Gerald J. Formosa. Vancouver, Canada: Skorba Publishers, 1975. 103p.

This volume studies the buildings of the Megalithic peoples, who achieved a very high level of consciousness and awareness through magic and mysticism. This mysticism is reflected in the forms of their buildings; for example, their use of the spiral to suggest the cycle of life, death and rebirth. Formosa claims that prehistoric man was fascinated by mathematics and astronomy, and used them to develop a greater awareness of the elements.

120 **The mortar wreck in Mellieha Bay, plans and soundings. A report on the 1967 campaign carried out on behalf of the National Museum of Malta.**
Honor Frost. London: Appetron Press, 1970. 40p.

An illustrated account based on a 1967 investigation of an ancient wreck in Mellieha Bay. It constituted a milestone in Maltese archaeological studies, since it was the first time that an important contribution to this branch of historical knowledge was financed by local sources.

121 **Malta in the ethnological complex of Europe.**
Lt. Col. Gayre of Gayre & Nigg. *St. Luke's Hospital Gazette*, vol. 6, no. 2 (1971), p. 83-98.

This was a public lecture given at the Royal University, Malta. The subjects covered included: description of the ethnic races; the prehistoric and historical evolution of the Maltese; the Tarxien Cemetery Period; the Conquest; the Order of St. John; and the synthesis of Maltese ethnology.

122 **Ancient Malta: a study of its antiquities.**
Harrison Lewis.   Gerrards Cross, Buckinghamshire, England: Colin Smythe, 1977. 168p. bibliog. illus.

A chronological survey of Malta's antiquities, which also describes as authentic-ally as possible the life and activities of ancient man during each period. The time of the Roman occupation of Malta has been reassessed here, as the conclusions of previous studies are somewhat unrealiable. A very useful reference work.

123 **Hal Millieri: a Maltese casale, its churches and paintings.**
Edited by Anthony Luttrell.   Valletta: Midsea Books, 1976. 143p. map.

A pioneering study of the deserted Hal Millieri casale, which also discusses late mediaeval Maltese painting, and the architecture of the typical Maltese rural church. Hall Millieri's annunciation chapel and wall paintings have been restored and preserved by the National Trust of Malta.

124 **Prehistoric finds.**
Francis S. Mallia.   Rome: University of Rome, 1965. p. 73-76.

This section of the book provides a brief account in English of the excavations at Tas-Silġ, a site which is noted for its prehistoric pottery. The author anlayses the dating of the 'fat lady' from Tas Silġ, at the Tarxien phase, ca.2400-2000 BC.

125 **Friendly refuge: a study of St. Paul's shipwreck and his stay in Malta.**
George H. Musgrave.   Heathfield, Sussex, England: Heathfield Publications, 1979. 120p. bibliog.

After careful examination of the evidence available, the author puts forward a new theory as to the site of St. Paul's shipwreck. He gives his reasons for this, and also outlines the characteristics of the age in which Paul lived, and describes the nature of the earliest churches.

126 **Prehistoric painted pottery in Malta.**
T. Eric Peet.   *Annals of Archaeology and Anthropology*, vol. 4, no. 4 (1911), p. 121-25.

This photographic study of archaeological finds reveals that Malta possesses a range of prehistoric pottery. Vase finds are undated and it is not known whether they are developments of prehistoric fabrics or whether they represent a totally different tradition.

127 **The megalithic art of the Maltese islands.**
Michael Ridley, foreword by Francis Mallia. Poole, Dorset,
England: Dolphin Press, 1976. 128p. map.

This descriptive inventory of Maltese megalithic art constitutes an important
advance in the study of one aspect of the islands' prehistoric culture which has in
the past received only sporadic and superficial attention. The author has brought
together all the relief carvings, the engravings and the paintings from both the
surface temples and the rock-cut Hypogeum.

128 **Malta and the Phoenicians.**
Lord Strickland, edited by Mabel Strickland, foreword by A.
Aquilina. Valletta: Progress Press, 1950. 32p.

The object of this treatise is to prove that the Maltese are not the descendants of
any Semitic or African race, but have close links with, and are descended from,
the Phoenicians.

129 **The prehistoric pottery found in the Hypogeum at Hal-Saflieni,
Casal Paula, Malta.**
N. Tagliaferro. *Annals of Archaeology and Anthropology*, vol. 3,
no. 1-2. (June 1910), 72p. 23 plates.

A clear and accurate description, supplemented by plates, of the pottery found at
the Hypogeum at Hal-Saflieni. This pottery has helped archaeologists to
determine the exact age not only of the Hypogeum but also of the other
megalithic monuments of the Maltese islands. As few of the vases were found
intact, most of the work relates to the twenty thousand potsherds found on site.

130 **Pre-historic Malta and Gozo.**
Celia Topp. Valletta: Progress Press, 1968. 52p.

A brief historical outline is followed by an account of: the cave of Ghar Dalam;
the geological formation of the islands and the problem of a land bridge; the
Neolithic temples of Tarxien; the Hypogeum of Hal-Saflieni; and the puzzling
presence of cart tracks on the island.

131 **National Museum of Malta: archaeological section.**
D. H. Trump. Valletta: National Museum Guide, 1960. 32p.
map.

A guide to the private archaeological collections which have now been brought
together in the National Museum of Malta.

132 **Skorba: excavations carried out on behalf of the National Museum
of Malta 1961-1963.**
D. H. Trump. Valletta: National Museum of Malta, 1966. 51p.
44 figs. 31 plates. map. Reports of the Research Committee of
the Society of Antiquaries of London, no. 22.

The excavation of Li Skorba in the north west of the island revealed the remains
of two adjacent temples which have since been extensively studied, and have

produced much useful evidence. Of even greater value was the information obtained from the archaeological remains of a village which had existed on the site until the construction of the temples. Material recovered from the successive levels of occupation has revealed in detail the early prehistory of the Maltese islands. With the help of a series of radiocarbon dates and comparable evidence from other areas, an assessment of the importance of the evidence recovered from Skorba to the prehistory of the whole central Mediterranean area is attempted. The volume is supplemented by numerous figures, plates and appendixes.

133　**Malta: an archaeological guide.**
D. H. Trump.　London: Faber & Faber, 1972. 171p. bibliog.

It is only in recent times, when tourism has come to play an important part in its economy, that Malta's archaeology has been considered one of its major assets. This work, unlike many guidebooks, provides a detailed discussion of the ancient sites. Meticulous work has been done at Tarxien and Mġarr but the island's past still bristles with unsolved archaeological problems.

134　**Prehistoric Malta, the Tarxien temples.**
Themistocles Zammit.　Cambride, England: Cambridge
University Press; London: Humphrey Milford, 1930. 127p. 4 maps.

An illustrative study of the Tarxien temples which illustrates the importance of Malta in early Mediterranean culture. The temples are one of the most interesting megalithic ruins for they represent a buried group of temples that flourished in the Stone Age and, after a considerable lapse of time, were utilised by a Bronze Age people for other purposes.

135　**The Copper Age temples of Hal-Tarxien, Malta.**
Themistocles Zammit.　Valletta: St. Francis Press, 1965. 36p.

A short, illustrated description of the monuments with plans. These monuments date from the Copper Age ca.2,200 BC, and were associated with ritual burials.

History

General

136 **Britain's crown jewels: Malta.**
Dunstan G. Bellanti. Valletta: Giov. Muscat, 1934. 57p.
An illustrated guide to, and history of, the Maltese islands which includes three
appendixes and a descriptive catalogue of the armoury of the Knights of St. John.

137 **The British Survey, June 1960. Malta: an Historical Survey.**
London: British Society for International Understanding, 1960.
20p. (Main Series, no. 135).
A general description of the historical and economic development of the island.

138 **Malta revisited: an appointment with history.**
Eric Gerada-Azzopardi. Valletta: Progress Press, 1984. 299p.
map. bibliog.
A vivid account of the events and personalities which have shaped the republic of
today. The text is highly readable and deliberately unacademic in tone. It is aimed
at the discerning visitor who is curious about the true character of the islands.

139 **The story of man in Malta.**
A. V. Laferla, introduction by Sir Harry Luke. Valletta:
Government Printing Press, 1958. 2 vols.
Volume one outlines the history of the islands and their inhabitants, from
prehistoric times to the expulsion of the French and the beginning of the English
occupation. In volume two the author traces the historical origins of some of the
old customs that still survive and links Malta's contemporary life with its rich
traditions.

140 **Outlines of Maltese history.**
S. Laspina. Valletta: A. C. Aquilina, 1971. 326p.

A general elementary survey of Malta from prehistoric to modern times. It contains documents and letters and is well illustrated. Three appendixes concern: extracts from Cicero's speech against Caius Verras; the declaration of rights of the inhabitants of Malta and Gozo; and the bishops of Malta and Gozo.

141 **Melitensia 1900-1975. Catalogue of the Exhibition held at St. John's Annexe, Valletta, June 3-15, 1975.**
Giovanni Mangion. Valletta: Malta Historical Society, 1975. 44p.

A work for scholars and historians. The exhibition was one of the major activities organized by the Malta Historical Society on the occasion of its 25th anniversary. Various sections cover: Maltese historiography; journals of historical interest; bibliography and methodology; general history; prehistory and ancient history; social and economic history; religious history; history of art and architecture; literary and linguistic history; the Second World War; and towns and villages.

142 **Melita Historica.**
Floriana, Malta: Malta Historical Society, 1952- . annual.

Covers the social, political, military, legal, architectural and natural history of Malta. The journal also contains reports of the publications and activities of the Malta Historical Society and includes articles in English and Italian.

143 **Malta.**
Bernard Nantet. Boulogne, France: Editions Delroisse. new ed. 1981. 195p. bibliog.

A lavishly illustrated account of Maltese history. The text is in English, French and German. There are six chapters entitled: 'Everything begins at Ghardalam'; 'The archipelago of giants'; 'Prehistory'; 'The people who came from the sea'; 'The Knights of Malta'; and 'The English and Maltese independence'.

144 **The Mediterranean.**
André Siegfried translated from the French by Doris Hemming. London: Jonathan Cape, 1948. 221p.

This discussion of the importance of the Mediterranean to British policy is suitable for both the specialist and the general reader. It includes references to Malta.

145 **L'Istorja Ta' Malta: Maltese history: what future?**
Edited by Ann Williams, Roger Villa Bonavita. Msida, Valletta: Malta University Press, 1974. 177p.

A compilation of papers in Italian, English and Maltese, which were presented at a conference in 1971, entitled 'Maltese history: what future?' The English contributions cover history books as teaching aids and public, private and local records in Malta.

146 **Malta – the Maltese islands and their history.**
Themistocles Zammit.   Valletta: A. C. Aquilina, 1952. 437p.
map. bibliog.

A comprehensive popular account of the history of the Maltese islands prior to
1885. The work has twenty chapters, twenty-four appendixes and forty-four
illustrations.

Pre 16th century

147 **Studies in Maltese history.**
P. F. Bellanti.   Valletta: Empire Press, 1924. 174p.

Part one of this work covers Maltese history in the first three centuries AD and
part two deals with the 4th and 5th centuries. It contains over eighty illustrations
of tombs. Several of the tombs were Christian and they retain many of the
features of Phoenician pagan tombs, as the people were recent converts to
Christianity.

148 **The sword and the scimitar: the saga of the Crusades.**
Ernle Bradford.   London: Victor Gollancz, 1974. 240p. 2 maps.
22 plates. bibliog.

A detailed account of the Crusades, which were undertaken by European
Christians between the 11th and the 14th centuries, in an attempt to recover the
Holy Land from the Moslems. The Crusades had a devestating effect on the
Mediterranean area, including Malta.

149 **Corsairs of Malta and Barbary.**
Peter Earle.   London: Sidgwick & Jackson, 1970. 307p. bibliog.

Based on original research in Malta, this is a comparative study of the Malta and
Barbary corsairs. The Barbary corsairs are quite well known to historians. They
were Moslems based in North Africa, who raided the ships and coastline of
Christian Europe. Less well documented is the fact that they were paralleled by a
similar Christian group, based in Malta and Italy, who raided Moslem ships and
the Mediterranean coastline. This study includes an account of five different
corsairs.

150 **Malta and the Aragonese Crown 1282-1530.**
A. T. Luttrell. *Journal of the Faculty of Arts*, vol. 3, no. 1 (1965),
p. 1-9.

An academic article outlining the role that Malta played in the spread of
Catalano-Aragonese power in the Mediterranean area.

151 **Mediaeval Malta: studies on Malta before the Knights.**
Edited by Anthony T. Luttrell. London: British School at Rome, 1975. 232p.

The history of mediaeval Malta has yet to be written in detail. These illustrated articles provide only a partial summary of events. The topics covered include: mediaeval and Renaissance architecture; lost villages and hamlets; Norman legends; Henry, Count of Malta (1203-30); and the Secrezia and royal patrimony in Malta between 1240 and 1450.

The Siege of Malta (1565)

152 **The true depiction of the investment and attack suffered by the island of Malta at the hands of the Turks in the year of our Lord 1565.**
Matteo Perez d'Aleccio, translation and notes by D. J. Calnan. Valletta: Progress Press, 1965. 70p.

This is the third edition of the illustrated sixteen folio war report, which first appeared in Rome in 1582. Its aim was to publicize the great victory of the Knights of St. John over the Turks throughout the Christian world.

153 **Malta in 1565, some recommendations.**
B.W. Blouet. *Journal of the Faculty of Arts*, vol. 3, no. 1 (1965), p. 8-21.

A reconsideration, in the light of new documentary evidence, of th 1565 Siege of Malta.

154 **The Great Siege of Malta, 1565.**
Ernle Bradford. London: Hodder & Stoughton, 1961. 256p. bibliog.

One of the few works in English dealing with the Great Siege of 1565, this is a readable and lucid account. Malta, then one of the eastern-most bastions of Christendom, was attacked by the Turks with 200 ships and 40,000 men. The island was defended by six or seven hundred Knights of St. John, along with 9,000 men.

155 **The Siege of Malta 1565.**
Francesco Balbi di Correggio, translated from the Spanish by Major H. A. Balbi, foreword by Sir Harry Luke. Copenhagen: Captain O. F. Gollcher & Dr. O. Rostock, 1961. 227p.

Correggio provides an interesting account of his experiences as a soldier during the Siege of Malta. The volume also includes estimates of the number of knights who died during the Siege and the number who survived.

156   **The Siege of Malta 1565.**
      Ian Colin Lochhead, T. F. R. Barling.   London: Literary Services
      and Production, 1970. 63p. bibliog.

A very readable account of the Order of St. John and its defence of Malta against
the Turks in 1565. The authors provide a vivid and authentic picture of the
knights, their island fortress and their foes. The narrative is both lively and
succinct, and the work includes a number of drawings and reproductions of
pictures of the Great Siege.

157   **The shield of Europe: the life and times of La Valette.**
      Bridget Cassar Borg Olivier.   Valletta: Progress Press, 1977.
      205p. map. bibliog.

La Valette, the Grand Master of the Order of St. John, led the defence of Malta
at the Great Siege. This factual account aims to provide a balanced view of his
character, unlike previous works which have focused almost exclusively on his
admirable qualities. This volume also discusses the history of the knights between
the years 1515 and 1568. The author stresses the importance of the siege which
prevented the expansion of the Ottoman Empire.

158   **A new history of the war in Malta (1565) translated into Italian
      from the original Latin of Celio Secondo Curione by Dr. Emanuele
      F. Mizzi.**
      A. Granville Pacha (English version).   Rome: Tipografia
      Leonina, 1928. 163p.

A concise, unbiased account of the Siege of Malta, which includes a biographical
sketch of the principal people who were involved in it.

16th–17th century

159   **The earliest description of Malta (Lyons 1536).**
      Jean Quintin d'Autun, translation and notes by Horatio C. R.
      Vella.   Sliema, Malta: De Bono Enterprises, 1980. 102p. map.
      bibliog.

Aimed at both the scholar and the general reader, this is the first annotated
translation of Abbé Jean Quintin d'Autun's description of Malta. Historians have
attached great importance to this document and to Vella's interpretation of it.
Extensive notes are provided, as well as indexes of Latin and Greek words and
ancient sources. See also item no. 162.

160 **Town planning in Malta 1530-1798.**
B. W. Blouet. *Town Planning Review* vol. 25, no. 3 (1964), p. 183-94.

This illustrated account opens with the reluctance of the knights to invest in a new fortress for the island, and ends with the rapid growth of settlements which took place around the end of the eighteenth century. In 1530, only 10% of the population lived in towns; by 1798 this figure had risen to 50%. Malta's economic life was by that time centred on the towns, which served as fortresses, naval bases and administrative centres.

161 **Gian Francesco Abela: essays in his honour by members of the 'Malta Historical Society' on the occasion of the third centenary of his death (1655-1955).**
Valletta: Department of Information, 1961. 110p.

Two of the essays in this volume to commemorate the death of the Maltese historian Abela, are in Italian but the remainder are in English and cover such subjects as: Abela's life and career; the influence of his work; Abela and the Maltese language; the topography of Malta in Abela's time; the natural history of Malta; and Maltese folklore.

162 **The first printed description of Malta, Lyons 1536.**
E. P. Leopardi. *Scientia*, vol. 15 (1949), p. 52-61. map.

A fascinating analysis of Abbé Jean Quintin d'Autun's *The earliest description of Malta* (q.v.) which was published in Lyons in 1536, and is almost certainly the first printed pamphlet dealing exclusively with the Maltese islands. The map in the article is a copy of one of the first printed maps of Malta.

163 **The nobles of Malta 1530-1800.**
John Montalto. Valletta: Midsea Books, 1979. 415p. bibliog.

This is the first attempt to deal with the fascinating subject of the Maltese nobility within the general context of the island's history. The author is neither for nor against the nobility, although he stresses the fact that they are an integral part of Malta's heritage. He obtained his material from private archives belonging to the noble families and from public collections. This volume covers the origins of the nobility; their links with the Order of St. John, with the grand masters, the bishops and the inquisitors, and their involvement in the defence of the island. It ends with a discussion of freemasonry and the role of the nobility during the brief French occupation. The work contains many illustrations, colour plates and a list of tables.

164 **The book of deliberations of the Venerable Tongue of England 1523-1567.**
Edited by H. P. Scicluna. Valletta: Empire Press, 1949. 98p. bibliog.

This work provides a history of the Order of the Venerable Tongue, a masonic order which originated in Malta. It contains an historical introduction, an index of names, a glossary and notes, as well a four pages reproduced in fascimile from the original.

165 **An Elizabethan-Ottoman conspiracy.**
Andrew P. Vella.   Msida, Valletta: Malta University Press, 1972.
168p.
The fascinating story of a conspiracy which, if successful, would have led to the English gaining a vital foothold in Malta 220 years before British rule was in fact established. The author examines the evidence which suggests that some Englishmen, allegedly in the service of Queen Elizabeth I and her Privy Council, collected information on the island's water suply, prepared or acquired plans and drawings of forts and castles, and corresponded with other English agents resident in the Levant. It is alleged that Queen Elizabeth I was secretly planning to capture Malta in league with the Ottoman Turks. Documents and illustrations are used to support these theories.

166 **The Tribunal of the Inquisition in Malta.**
Andrew P. Vella.   Msida, Valletta: Malta University Press, 1973.
71p. (Royal University of Malta Historical Studies, no. 1).
Intended for both the specialist and the general reader, this is the story of the Tribunal of the Inquisition. Special judges were appointed to deal with crimes against the faith, and they imposed very high penalties on offenders. Such penalties were defined by canonical procedures statutes.

167 **Malta under the Cotoners 1660-1680.**
Winston L. Zammit.   Hamrun, Malta: Lux Press, 1980. 97p.
Raphael Cotoner was Grand Master of Malta from 1660 to 1663. He was succeeded by his brother Nicholas, who held power for the next sixteen and a half years. Nicholas had to contend with many problems concerning religion and national security, but proved himself to be a strong and successful ruler. This is a valuable work providing a mature and perceptive analysis of the period. Many original sources in the National Library of Malta were used.

18th–20th century

168 **The history of freemasonry in the district of Malta from 1800 to the present time.**
A. M. Broadley.   London: George Kenning, 1880. 122p.
This detailed account of freemasonry in Malta is unsurpassed, despite the fact that it is now over 100 years old.

169 **The nobles of Malta as at present existing.**
George Crispo-Barbaro.   Valletta: Vuglisevich, 1883. 8p.
A good account of the Maltese nobility in the early 1880's, written in a very patriotic style. It is a useful guide for those who wish to know who Malta's nobles are, and the author also hoped it would prevent people from using titles to which they had no legitimate claim. The text is in English and Italian.

170 The French in Malta.

Victor F. Denaro. *Scientia.* vol. 29 (1963), 65p.

This work covers the period 1798 to 1800 and includes items on administration, treasures, education, press freedom, goldsmiths, Church-state relations, and the Maltese insurrection against the French.

171 Birth pangs of a nation: Manwel Dimech's Malta (1860-1921).

Henry Frendo. Hamrun, Malta: Mediterranean Publications, 1972. 167p. bibliog.

A study of the life and work of Manwel Dimech, a Maltese political thinker and activist, who was prepared to use illegal means to pursue his aims. In his own lifetime he was largely unsuccessful in his attempts to introduce his ideas of society and nationhood, but, as this study points out, he maintained his social and political idealism, despite many set-backs.

172 Some official enactments under the early British rule in Malta.

Joseph Galea. *Sundial* vol. 4, no. 10 (Oct.1949), p. 8.

A lecture given at the Royal University of Malta in 1949. It throws a great deal of light on the way of life and social conditions in Malta in the first two decades of the 19th century.

173 Malta: historical sketches.

Michael Galea. Valletta: the author, 1970. 64p. bibliog.

A collection of essays, focusing on particular moments in Malta's history. There are detailed descriptions of celebrations and festivities, which illuminate Maltese behaviour, and life and customs at different periods of history. The subjects covered include: the Great Siege monument; the first visit to Malta by a reigning British monarch; Malta's two national assemblies; the first parliament war memorial; and VE Day celebrations on the island.

174 Malta: more historical sketches.

Michael Galea. Zabbar, Malta: Veritas Press, 1971. 90p. bibliog.

A unique and fascinating study of 19th-century Maltese social history, illustrated with black-and-white photographs. It covers the visits to the island of Queen Victoria in 1838, William Thackeray in 1844 and Giuseppe Garibaldi in 1864. It also describes Maltese carnivals, the first train journey on the island in 1883, the celebrations for Queen Victoria's Jubilee, Malta's first general elections (1849), and the inauguration of the Malta Opera House in 1866.

175 Maltese legal history under British rule 1801-1836.

Hugh W. Harding. Valletta: Progress Press, 1968. 421p.

This history of Maltese legislation under British rule begins with the appointment of Charles Cameron in May 1801 as Her Majesty's First Civil Commissioner for Malta. The work ends with Ponsonby's Lieutenant Governorship in 1836. During the period under discussion, a great deal of new legislation was enacted and much more was contemplated. Legislative reform, however, was often retarded and impeded by a variety of causes and British policy was cautious.

176 **A history of Malta during the period of the French and British occupations 1798-1815.**
Edited by William Hardman, introduction and notes by J. Holland Rose. London: Longmans, Green, 1909. 657p.

A collection of English and foreign documents which present Britain's activities in Malta from 1798 to 1815 and describe the circumstances leading to the attack and capture of the islands by the French Republic. The book also covers the subsequent naval and military operations by British and Maltese forces, aided by their Portugese and Neapolitan allies, which resulted in Britain obtaining and securing possession of Malta. The volume includes four detailed appendixes.

177 **What happened to the Empress?**
Robert Ingham. Hamrun, Malta: St. Joseph's Institute, 1949. 80p.

An interesting account of the visit to Malta of Her Imperial Majesty the Dowager Empress of Russia in April 1919. It is written in an anecdotal style.

178 **British Malta. vol. I. 1800-1872.**
A. V. Laferla, introduction by Sir Harry Luke. Valletta: Royal Malta Library, 1938. 285p. bibliog.

This volume considers the capture of Malta by the British in 1800 and examines the beginnings of modern Maltese politics. It also refers to educational and ecclesiastical developments down to 1872. A second volume, edited by G. Zarb Adami, with an introduction by H. P. Scicluna (Valletta: Aquilina for the Royal Malta Library, 1947. 238p. bibliog.) has also appeared. It is a remarkably unbiased account, based on hitherto unexamined primary sources. The author adopts the maxim that the art of good government can be learned through the study of history. The volume covers Malta's history from 1872 to 1921, the year when the island was granted dominion government status.

179 **The Nile Campaign, Nelson and Napoleon in Egypt.**
Christopher Lloyd. New York: Barnes & Noble; Newton Abbot, England: David & Charles, 1973. 120p.

Napoleon's conquest of Malta in 1798 is covered on p. 10-25 of this volume, and its capture two years later by the British fleet under Admiral Nelson is studied on p. 96-103. The eye witness accounts reproduced in this work are particularly interesting.

180 **The petition of the Maltese to the House of Commons: a letter addressed to H. M. Principal Secretary of State for the Colonies by one of the elected members of the Council of Government of Malta.**
Valletta: Albion Press, 1880. 30p.

This letter outlines the anger of the Maltese at their not being represented in their own government.

181 **Princess Olga my mother, her life and times. The Grand Duke Michael Alexandrovitch abdication to the throne of Russia.**
Princess Nathalie Poutiatine.   Valletta: Gulf Publishing, 1982. 240p.

Princess Olga was in Malta from 1945 until her death in 1965, and her exile on the island is covered on p. 205-40 of this volume.

182 **Some unpublished documents on Gozo (1793-1818).**
J. Cassar Pullicino.   *Scientia* vol. 25 nos. 2-3 (1959), p. 87-138.

The documents concerned belonged to a private collection and were printed in the hope of encouraging further historical research on Gozo. They deal with three main events, namely: the invasion of Gozo by the French and the subsequent rising of the Gozitans; the administration of Gozo during the blockade; and the governorship of Gozo during the first years of British rule. The text is in English and Italian.

183 **Britain in Malta.**
Harrison Smith.   Valletta: Progress Press, 1953. 2 vols. bibliog.

Volume one entitled *Constitutional development of Malta in the 19th century*, provides an impartial analysis of Malta's problems while under British rule. It covers constitutional reforms, the language question, education and the relationship between Church and State. The study emphasizes the constitutional developments which resulted from the 1887 decision to grant some degree of self-government to the islands under the pioneering work of Lord Strickland. Volume two, *Italian influence on British policy in Malta*, claims that the influence of Italy became the most significant factor in Maltese history in this period. In this work, the author has consulted a wide range of primary sources and has also utilized secondary sources when necessary.

184 **Lord Strickland: servant of the crown.**
Harrison Smith.   Amsterdam: Koster Publishers, 1983. 524p. bibliog.

A scholarly study which draws on many primary and secondary sources. Strickland played an important part in Maltese politics, beginning in 1887, when he helped to frame the Maltese constitution. Later, he formed the Anglo-Maltese Party, and was prime minister and minister of justice in the Maltese coalition government of 1927-30. This volume covers the whole of Strickland's long and eventful life and includes appendixes which provide extracts from his addresses and speeches.

185 **A collection of essays on Malta 1923-54.**
Mabel Strickland.   Valletta: Progress Press, 1955. 111p.

A small volume of essays, covering thirty years of Maltese history. Titles include: 'Has England forgotten Malta?'; 'A colony of Carthage'; 'Malta'; 'Life in Malta during the Siege'; 'Malta: the key to the Mediterranean'; and 'Malta: fortress of freedom'. A drawback to this publication is that there is some repetition in the subject matter, but the essays, together with ten appendixes, provide a useful insight into Malta's recent history.

186 **An unpublished diary of Queen Adelaide's visit to Malta in 1838.**
Scientia vol. 29. (1963), p. 99-116.
A very detailed and informative illustrated account of the royal visit. Queen
Adelaide (1792-1849) was the wife of the British monarch, William IV.

Second World War

187 **The Battle of Malta.**
Joseph Attard.   London: William Kimber, 1980. 252p. 2 maps.
bibliog.
The author's own experiences and those of other eye witnesses are used to assess
the impact of the Battle of Malta on the people. The account was written in order
to rectify the inaccuracies and omissions of other records. It covers the Siege of
Malta, which lasted from June 1940 to September 1943, and emphasizes the
combined efforts of the British and Maltese armed services, the police, the
Passive Defences and the Maltese people.

188 **The ship busters.**
Ralph Barker.   London: Chatto & Windus, 1957. 220p.
The story of the RAF torpedo bombers including an account of a series of strikes
from Malta in 1942 and the June Malta convoy. A very graphic and readable
account.

189 **One man's window: an illustrated account of ten weeks of war,**
Malta April 13 to June 21, 1942.
Dennis Barnham.   London: William Kimber, 1956. 201p.
An extensively illustrated account, based on a detailed diary.

190 **Malta invicta.**
Bartimeus.(*pseud.*)   London: Chatto & Windus, 1943. 32p.
A booklet written to commemorate the award of the George Cross to the people
of Malta as an appreciation of their bravery in the Second World War. It is
supplemented by excellent photographs taken during the war. Bartimeus was the
pseudonym of Captain Lewis Ritchie.

191 **The second great siege, Malta 1940-43.**
Charles J. Boffa.   Hamrun, Malta: St. Joseph's Institute, 1970.
138p. bibliog.
A brief survey that emphasizes the courage and resourcefulness of the Maltese,
who withstood three years of air raids and hunger. It was written in order to
prevent people forgetting the horror of war. Another interesting volume on this
subject is *Siege: Malta 1940-1943* by Ernle Bradford (London: Hamish Hamilton,

1985. 247p. bibliog.) The work draws on a wide range of sources, including first hand accounts, and also utilizes new research which demonstrates Malta's importance as a centre for the reception of information from the British intelligence service *Ultra*.

192 **Deportation 1942: the internment and deportation of Maltese nationalists.**
R. Bondin. Valletta: Rama Publications, 1980. 139p. bibliog.
An account of a little known aspect of Maltese history. In 1942, ninety Maltese nationalists were interned by the British government and fifty were deported to Uganda. This volume studies the types of people who were interned and describes their treatment during interment. It also deals with the incitement of the press, the protests and appeals of the internees and their struggle to prove the illegality of deportation.

193 **Spitfires over Malta.**
Paul Brennan, Ray Hesselyn, Henry Bateson, foreword by Lord Londonderry. London: Jarrolds, 1944. 96p.
An illustrated account of the air war over Malta, during the Second world War, written only months after it took place.

194 **Senglea during the Second Great War 1940-44.**
Emmanuel Brincat. Valletta: Progress Press, 1979. 107p.
An account by the parish priest in Senglea, of life in the town during the Second World War.

195 **The epic of Malta.**
Foreword by Winston Churchill, text by Lewis Ritchie. London: Odhams Press, 1944. 128p.
This illustrated collection of articles is an acknowledgement of the great contribution which the Maltese made to the Allied victory in the Second World War.

196 **The siege of Malta, 1940-1943.**
J. M. Debono. Hamrun, Malta: Lux Press, 1950. 21p.
A long poem describing the Second World War siege of Malta, much of which was written during the bombardment.

197 **An island beleaguered.**
F. S. De Domenico. Valletta: Giov. Muscat, 1946. 187p.
An illustrated history, written by an eyewitness, of the endurance and courage shown by the Maltese in the Second World War. It is based on the author's immediate impressions.

198 **The air battle for Malta: the diaries of a fighter pilot.**
James Douglas-Hamilton, introduction by Laddie
Lucas. Edinburgh: Mainstream Publishing, 1981. 208p. bibliog.

This illustrated account is based on the official diary of the Royal Air Force's 603
Squadron, and on the personal diary of its commander.

199 **Malta, the triumphant years, 1940-43.**
George Hogan. London: Robert Hale, 1978. 192p. map. bibliog.

This volume is based on the author's recollections of the war, but it also draws on
other accounts such as Leslie Oliver's *Malta besieged* (London: Hutchinson, 1943.
225p.), Sybil Dobbie's *Grace under Malta* (London: Lindsay Drummond, 1944.
230p.) and Francis Gerard's *Malta magnificent* (London: Cassell, 1943, 192p.).
Hogan provides a colourful and dramatic narrative, which captures the unfailing
courage and spirit of the people during this difficult time.

200 **Malta victory: Yeoman on the George Cross island.**
Robert Jackson. London: Arthur Barker, 1980. 173p. map.

A racy, journalese account of the war years, centred on the exploits of the
fictional character of Spitfire pilot, Flight Lieutenant George Yeoman.

201 **Besieged: the World War II ordeal of Malta, 1940-42.**
Charles A. Jellison. Hanover, New Hampshire: University Press
of New England, 1985. 320p. 2 maps.

This fine narrative is a lively and often moving account of a vital period of Malta's
history. It describes the effects of the bombardment on the people of the island,
who were deprived of necessities such as food and medicine, for over two years.
During this time, the island was subjected to some of the heaviest sustained
bombing ever unleashed upon such a small area.

202 **Lest we forget 'Santa Marija' 1942: a tribute to Malta convoy heroes.**
Sunday Times of Malta (Aug. 1967), p. 1-11.

An emotive and patriotic illustrated account of the convoys.

203 **When Malta stood alone 1940-43.**
Joseph Miccallef. Valletta: Interprint, 1981. 190p. map.

In the space of two and a half years, Malta suffered 3,340 air raids, in which over
14,000 tons of bombs were dropped. 1,500 people were killed, 2,000 seriously
injured and 9,000 premises were destroyed or badly damaged. This volume uses
official reports and records, documents and eyewitness accounts to tell the story
of Malta's endurance during this time.

204 **Hero – the falcon of Malta: life of George 'Buzz' Beurling.**
Brian Nolan. London: William Blackwood, 1982. 201p. bibliog.

An account of the career of the Canadian pilot George Beurling, who shot down
twenty-seven planes in just fourteen days in Malta. By the end of the war, this
total had risen to thirty-one. The work is based on public and personal records.

205 **The siege within the walls: Malta 1940-43.**
Stewart Perowne.   London: Hodder & Stoughton, 1970. 192p.
bibliog.
An illustrated, popular account of Malta at war. It covers the convoys, the air
raids, and the resolve of the Maltese.

206 **Night strike from Malta: 830 Squadron R N and Rommel's convoys.**
Kenneth Poolman.   London: Jane's Publishing Company, 1980.
208p. map.
An illustrated survey for the layman of the war in Malta, with particular reference
to the year 1942.

207 **The Mediterranean, its role in America's foreign policy.**
William Reitzel.   New York: Harcourt, Brace & Company, 1948.
195p.
The importance of Malta in American strategy, during the Second World War is
discussed in this study.

208 **Malta convoy.**
Peter Shankland, Anthony Hunter.   London: Collins, 1961. 256p.
bibliog.
A vivid recreation of the vital convoy of August 1942. It uses official documents
from both the Allied and the Axis Powers. A second edition of this volume has
been published (London: Fontana, 1969. 192p.)

209 **Pedestal: the Malta convoy of August, 1942.**
Peter C. Smith.   London: William Kimber, 1970. 208p. 9 maps.
bibliog.
This valuable study provides a balanced picture of the Malta convoy operations of
1940-42. The Mediterranean was the scene of some very fierce fighting during the
Second World War, largely because it was so important for the Royal Navy to
keep possession of Malta.

210 **Malta-Floriana in wartime: a collection of essays 1940-1945.**
Emmanuel S. Tonna.   Malta: The Author, 1969. 112p.
A collection of recollections illustrated with fine photographs.

211 **The conferences at Malta and Yalta 1945.**
US Department of State.   Westport, Connecticut: Greenwood
Press, 1976. 1,032p. bibliog.
A reprint of a 1955 edition published by the US Government Printing Office in
Washington DC, issued in the series Foreign Relations of the United States
(FRUS) Diplomatic Papers, and as Department of State Publication 6199. At the
Malta Conference, attended by Roosevelt and Churchill, post-war relations with
the Soviet Union were discussed.

212   **War Dead of the British Commonwealth and Empire. The Register of the names of those who fell in the 1939-45 War and are buried in cemeteries in Malta, G.C.**
London: Imperial War Graves Commission, 1959. 87p. map.

Knights of St. John

213 The shield and the sword: the Knights of St. John.
Ernle Bradford.   London: Hodder & Stoughton, 1972. 245p.
bibliog.

This volume, which is suitable for the layman, captures the drama and excitement of the knights' story. It is a concise and moving historical account, with good quality engravings and photographs. The military success of the knights, as well as their courage, idealism and commitment to Christianity are thoroughly documented. Appendixes provide a list of grand masters, a military glossary and a short history of the order after losing Malta to the French, in 1798.

214 Bulletin of the Sovereign Order of Saint John of Jerusalem-Knights Hospitallers of Malta.
Floriana, Malta: Grand Priory of Malta, 1964- . quarterly.

This periodical contains articles on the history of the order, including: its fortifications and pilgrim hostels; biographies of grand masters; and local and foreign news of the order's activities.

215 The Order of St. John in Malta: an historical sketch.
Lionel Butler.   In: *The Order of St. John in Malta*. Edited by
Mattia Preti.   Valletta: St. Paul's Press, 1971. 333p.

A brief outline of the history of the Knights of Malta, in seven parts. It was reprinted from the catalogue of the 13th Council of Europe Art Exhibition, which was held in Malta in 1970, and arranged by the government of Malta and the Council of Europe.

216   **Knights in durance.. A record of the carvings and inscriptions in the**
      dungeon of the Castle of St. Angelo in Malta together with an
      account of the knights confined therein between 1532 and 1670.
      Dennis Calnan.   Hamrun, Malta: St. Joseph's Institute, 1966. 57p.
      28 plates.

An account of the knights who were held prisoner in the dungeon of the Castle of
St. Angelo, including a list of the crimes they committed, and the manner of their
death. The volume also details the discovery of inscriptions and carvings on the
dungeons, and summarizes the author's subsequent research on the subject.
There is a useful glossary and some extremely clear photographs, which reveal the
high quality of the carvings.

217   **The last of the crusaders: the Knights of St. John in Malta in the**
      18th century.
      Roderick Cavaliero.   London: Hollis & Carter, 1960. 298p. map.
      bibliog.

The last years of the order are described in this volume. The knights had ruled the
island since 1530 and formed a very efficient city state, but by the 18th century
they were in decline.

218   **Constitutions of the Sovereign and Military Order of the Knights**
      Hospitaller of St. John of Jerusalem also known as the Knights of
      Malta.
      In conformity with the Code of Canon Law.   Rome: Sovereign &
      Military Order of St. John of Jerusalem, 1963. 38p.

This volume is divided into eight sections entitled: 'The nature and aims of the
order'; 'The erection of priories'; 'Government of the order'; 'Admission to the
order'; 'Obligations and privileges'; 'Transfer to another religious order'; 'On
leaving the order'; and 'Dismissal from the order'. It is a translation from Italian.

219   **Holy Infirmary: sketches.**
      A. Critien.   Hamrun, Malta: Lux Press, 1946. 50p.

An illustrated survey of the Holy Infirmary, which was one of the most important
institutions to be established by the order. The author provides coverage of the
Holy Infirmary Dietary and the Holy Infirmary Plate.

220   **The Borg Holy Infirmary now the St. Scholastica Convent.**
      A. Critien.   Valletta: Empire Press, 1950. 36p.

A brief, illustrated history of the Borg Holy Infirmary, which was the first hospital
built in Malta by the Knights of St. John.

221   **Houses of the French knights in Valletta.**
      Victor F. Denaro.   *Revue de L'ordre Souverain Militaire de Malte*
      no. 3 (1958), p. 147-55.

An account of the houses of the *langues* of Provence, France and Auvergne,
which were first established in 1570.

222 **The spiritual heritage of the Sovereign Military Order of Malta.**
François Ducaud-Bourget adapted from the French by Geza
Grosschmid, Primitivo Colombo.   Vatican City: Tipografia
Poliglotta Vaticana, 1958. 239p. bibliog.
This volume outlines the activities of the Order of Malta in the 20th century.

223 **Knights of St. John.**
Gerhart Ellul (*pseud.*), translated by J. Bockett-Pugh.   London:
Lutterworth Press, 1958. 139p. map.
This work relates the history of the Knights of St. John in the Holy Land, on the
island of Rhodes and in Malta. The author provides an appreciation of the
Knights' devotion to the ideals of charity, self-sacrifice and service to mankind.

224 **Knights of Malta: a gallery of portraits.**
Claire Elaine Engel.   London: Allen & Unwin, 1963. 204p.
bibliog.
A discussion of the knights as individuals, rather than as members of the order.
During the 250 years of its existence in Malta, the order produced a large number
of outstanding and sometimes eccentric men.

225 **The Sovereign Order of Malta.**
Joseph Galea.   Valletta: Malta News Publication, 1958. 30p.
An appreciation of the order, written in response to a revival of interest in it,
which emphasizes the knights' courage, loyalty and forbearance.

226 **The old hospitals: the Order of St. John.**
Joseph Galea, Frederick F. Fenech.   *American Journal of Clinical
Pediatrics*, vol. 6, no. 12 (Dec. 1967), p. 728-34.
A comprehensive, illustrated survey of the Sacred Infirmary at Valletta.

227 **The history of the Order of Malta.**
John Galvin.   Dublin: Irish Association of the Sovereign Military
Order of Malta, 1979. 72p.
Chapter three (p. 29-37) of this volume is relevant to Malta.

228 **The knightly twilight: a glimpse at the chivalric and nobility
underworld.**
Lt. Col. Gayre of Gayre & Nigg.   Valletta: Lochore Enterprises,
1973. 172p.
A fascinating account, with heraldic drawings and insignia, of people who make
false claims to be members of a chivalric order in Malta.

229 **The role and responsibilities of the Order of Malta in the world of today.**
Quintin Jermy Gwyn.   Rome: Palazzo Malta, 1968. 38p.
The text in English, French, German, Italian and Spanish, of an address which was given at the opening of a conference of Grand Priors and Presidents of National Associations in Rome in 1968.

230 **Some letters from the Archives of the Knights of St. John, preserved at Valletta, Malta.**
Gavin B. Henderson.   *Mariners Mirror*, vol. 32, no. 2 (1944), p. 96-104. (The Quarterly Journal of the Society for Nautical Research).
An absorbing account of a previously neglected source, namely the letters in the Archives of the Knights of St. John.

231 **A catalogue of the Foster Stearns Collection on the Sovereign Military Order of St. John of Jerusalem, called, of Malta.**
Oliver L. Kapsner.   Washington DC: Catholic University of America Library, 1955. 61p.
A very important collection of 281 items, which covers over 800 years of the Order's history and includes all the major works which have been published on the Knights of Malta, up to the year 1955.

232 **The Hospitallers' historical activities 1530-1630.**
Anthony Luttrell.   Extract from *Annales* no. 3 (1968), 13p.
Based on primary sources, this is a scholarly study of the Knights, from 1530 (the year in which they were granted sovereignty of Malta by the Holy Roman Emperor) to 1630. It includes a useful note on the Malta archives.

233 **The Hospitallers in Cyprus, Rhodes, Greece and the West, 1291-1440: collected studies.**
Anthony Luttrell.   London: Variorum Reprints, 1978. 394p.
Occasional references to Malta occur throughout this collection of articles.

234 **Description of the island of Malta and a brief treatise on knightly behaviour written by the noble knight Camillo Spreti in the year 1764.**
Translated from the Italian, introduced and annotated by Averil Mackenzie-Grieve.   Valletta: Library Committee O.S.J.J. 1950. 40p. (History Pamphlet, no. 4.)
Spreti's pamphlet shows his respect for the traditional chivalric values of the old aristocratic community of knights, and his disappointment that the Knights of Malta had become powerful property owners.

235 **Catalogue of the records of the Order of St. John of Jerusalem in the Royal Malta Library.**
J. Mizzi. Msida, Valletta: Malta University Press, 1970. vol. 2, part 1, Archives 73-83, 168p. Msida, Valletta: Malta University Press, 1973, vol. 2, part 2, Archives 84-87, 162p.

Written in English and Latin, the records of the Order constitute an accurate account of its history.

236 **Visit to Malta by His Most Eminent Highness The Prince and Grand Master of the Sovereign Military Hospitaller Order of St. John of Jerusalem of Rhodes and of Malta, June 1968.**
Fra' Angelo de Mojana. Valletta: [s.n.] 1968. 91p.

The story of Fra' Angelo's visit to Malta in 1968.

237 **The devotion of the Knights of Malta for Our Lady of Philermo.**
Edited by Nicholas Moroso, translated by G. B. Grosschmid, P. Colombo. Pittsburgh, Pennsylvania: Duquesne University Press, 1955. 29p.

An attempt to link 20th-century American Catholics with the great Catholic institutions of the past. The author emphasizes the important role of military religious orders, such as the Knights of Malta, in the development of the Christian virtues of charity and compassion.

238 **The seven year balance sheet of the Order of St. John of Jerusalem from 1 May 1778 to the end of April 1785.**
Chevalier Bosredon de Ransijat, introduction and glossary by Captain J. M. Wismayer. Naxxar, Malta: Universal Intelligence Data Bank of America (Europe) 1984. 79p.

This illustrated study of the seven year balance sheet of the Order, shows the material benefits to the Maltese of the knights' rule. The volume contains two appendixes.

239 **St. John's Gate: headquarters of the Order of St. John.**
London: St. John Ambulance Association, 1982. 24p.

The official guide to the collections housed in St. John's Gate London, which tell the history of the Order of St. John. The collection includes many documents, as well as shields, badges and armour.

240 **The Valletta armoury and a letter from Sir Guy Laking.**
Edward Sammut. *Scientia*, vol. 25, no. 1 (1959), p. 16.

The Valletta armoury is unique in that among the 5,700 pieces it houses there is not a single forgery. As a record of the armourers' art it is sufficiently comprehensive to rank among the most precious treasures bequeathed by the knights.

241 **The Order of St. John of Jerusalem.**
     Hannibal P. Scicluna.   Valletta: Government Printing Press, 1930.
     53p.
A brief account of the order's origin, organization and history.

242 **The Order of St. John of Jerusalem: a brief account of its origin,
     organisation and history and a short description of the historical,
     archaeological and picturesque places of interest in Malta and Gozo.**
     Hannibal P. Scicluna.   Floriana, Malta: Empire Press, 1969. 380p.
     bibliog.
A well-written and lavishly illustrated history of the Order of St. John, together
with a brief survey of the interesting sights of Malta and Gozo.

243 **The Sovereign Military Order of Malta, yesterday and today.**
     Rome: Stab. Tip DAPCo, 1956. 32p.
A descriptive account of the Order with many illustrations.

244 **The grand masters of the Soveriegn Order of St. John of Jerusalem
     Knights Hospitaller.**
     Gaston Tonna-Barthett.   Valletta: Russian Grand Priory of
     Malta, 1973. 96p.
This work is of particular value to the reader who is interested in engravings of
grand masters of the order. It contains a preface in Maltese, French, English and
Italian.

245 **Biography of the grand masters of the Sovereign Order of St. John
     of Jerusalem.**
     Gaston Tonna-Barthett.   Valletta: Russian Grand Priory of
     Malta,
     1974. 183p.
This extensively illustrated volume contains a brief history of all the grand masters
of the order.

246 **The insignia and medals of the Grand Priory of the Most Venerable
     Order of the Hospital of St. John of Jerusalem.**
     Charles W. Tozer.   London: J. B. Hayward, in association with
     the Orders and Medals Research Society and approved by the
     Order of St. John, 1975. 80p.
The first comprehensive study of the decorations and medals of the Order of St.
John, this volume also includes some brief notes on the history of the order.

247 **A short history of the Knights of the Sovereign and Military Order
of St. John of Jerusalem of Rhodes and of Malta (part I).**
Theodore Veevers-Thompson.   London: Association of British
Members of the Sovereign Military Order of Malta, 1956. 26p.

Chapter three of this volume (p. 19-25) provides a brief history of the Knights in
Malta.

248 **The history of the Knights of Malta.**
L'Abbé de Vertot.   London: G. Strahan, 1728. 2 vols.

These volumes discuss the process by which the religious aims of the knights were
united with, and finally overtaken by, their military ambitions. The work is
divided into fifteen books and contains many maps and engravings.

Genealogy and Heraldry

249 The family of Inguanez.

Marcel Dingli-Attard-Inguanez.   Valletta: Interprint, 1979. 2nd ed. 86p.

This volume, which was first published in 1888, includes a collection of documents on the Inguanez family, a poem by Carmel Inguanez, and an account of the legal aspects of heraldry. The Spanish family of Inguanez inherited the governorship of the Maltese islands until 1530, when Malta was granted to the Knights. The family's coat of arms is engraved on the inside of the Main Gate of Mdina.

250 The International Armorial Register. A Register of Armorial Bearings in current use with the names and addresses of the bearers and the authority for their use.

Edited by Marcel Dingli-Attard-Inguanez.   Independence, Missouri: Universal Intelligence Data Bank of America, 1984; Naxxar, Malta: Heraldry Society, 1984. 380p.

Specific references to Malta occur in the appendixes to this volume: on p. 363-4 there is an account of the Maltese nobility as recognized by the 1877 Royal Commission; and p. 364-67 contain a list of titles granted to individuals who were directly or indirectly connected with Malta.

251 Genealogical memoirs of the family of Strickland of Sizergh.

Henry Hornyold.   Kendal, England: Titus Wilson, 1928. 330p.

An illustrated account of the Strickland family, including its various branches. The family is notable for its long line of unbroken descent, its continued possession of the ancestral home, and for its loyalty to the Church and State. The earliest printed geneaological account of the Stricklands dates from 1777. This work is based on Walter Strickland's four-volume manuscript study of the family. The Stricklands are an English family, but have close links with Malta. Some of the family have lived there since the turn of the 20th-century.

Emigration and
Minorities

252 **Early Maltese emigration 1800-1914. (Men and means.)**
Lawrence E. Attard.   Valletta: Gulf Publishing, 1983. 54p.
bibliog.

A very interesting and important study which deals principally with Maltese
emigration to Anglo Saxon countries, although one chapter studies the attempt to
create a Maltese colony in Brazil. Attard argues that one of the main reasons for
emigration from Malta has always been unemployment.

253 **The determinants of modern Maltese emigration.**
E. P. Delia.   *International Migration*, vol. 20, nos. 1-2 (1982), p.
11-25.

The author identifies various subgroups in the flow of emigration from Malta, and
demonstrates that the findings of demographers Russell King and Huw R. Jones,
which attribute Maltese emigration to sociodemographic factors and not to
economic factors, need qualification. Economic factors, both within Malta and the
recipient countries from 1948 to 1975, played a significant part in emigration.
However, the demographic conditions influencing the numbers of people
emigrating should not be underestimated. The article is based on Malta census
data and other pirmary sources.

254 **Modern emigration from Malta: a liability?**
E. P. Delia.   *Hyphen*, vol. 3, no. 4 (1982), p. 141-64.

In the 19th century emigration represented one of the solutions to Malta's
demographic and economic problems, but it was not until after the Second World
War that the Maltese government actively encouraged emigration. The author
analyses the reasons for recent emigration, and evluates its contribution to
populaton control, the reduction of unemployment and the saving of capital
resources. He also discusses the behavioural characteristics of the 'typical'
Maltese emigrant.

52

255   **Maltese in London: a case-study in the erosion of ethnic
consciousness.**
Geoffrey Dench.   London: Routledge & Kegan Paul, 1975. 302p.
bibliog.

The Maltese were among the first colonial citizens to embark on a large-scale
migration to Britain after the Second World War. The majority of the migrants
wanted to be absorbed into the British community and sought individual
assimilation; and there tended to be problems for the few who did not accept the
British way of life.

256   **The effects of return migration on a Gozitan village.**
Russell King, Alan Strachan.   *Human Organization*, vol. 39, no. 2
(1980), p. 175-79.

This article surveys returning migrants to the village of Qala on Gozo in 1978, and
concludes that nonmigrants are more integrated into village life than are
returnees.

257   **Malta and the Maltese: a study in 19th century migration.**
Charles A. Price.   Melbourne, Australia: Georgian House, 1954.
Reprinted, New York: AMS Press, 1977. 272p. bibliog.

In the 19th century, Malta became so overpopulated that some emigration was
inevitable. This volume studies the social, political and economic factors which
influenced emigration and discusses the problems of adjustment which the
migrants had to face. These problems included loneliness, dietetic prejudices, and
tenacity to the Roman Catholic faith. Price argues that there was a lack of
initiative in the educated migrants, as they tended to rely on their money to solve
their problems, instead of making an effort to improve their way of life.

258   **The Jews of Malta.**
Cecil Roth.   London: Transactions of the Jewish Historical
Society, 1931. p.187-251.

Aimed at the specialist, this paper outlines the history of the Jews in Malta,
including their relations with other minority groups and with the Maltese.

Language

General

259 **A comparative study in mixed Maltese.**
Joseph Aquilina. Hamrun, Malta: Lux Press, 1949. 29p.
A brief work which illustrates the interrelationship between the development of
the Maltese language and the political and cultural history of the country.

260 **Maltese as a mixed language.**
Joseph Aquilina. *Journal of Semitic Studies*, vol. 3, no. 1 (1958),
p. 58-79.
This article outlines the history of the Maltese language and provides a linguistic
analysis.

261 **Papers in Maltese linguistics.**
Joseph Aquilina. Msida, Valletta: Malta University Press, 1970.
240p.
A vivid presentation of the Maltese language. It provides a detailed and scholarly
discussion of: Maltese semantics and lexicography; phonetic changes; the links
between race and language; and the origins of Maltese place names. The volume
also surveys systems of Maltese orthography and indicates the link which Maltese
forms between the Semitic and Romance languages.

262 **The structure of Maltese: a study in mixed grammar and vocabulary.**
Joseph Aquilina.   Msida, Valletta: Malta University Press, 1973. 358p. bibliog.

Aquilina provides a detailed phonological analysis of the Maltese language and emphasizes its mixed origins. Maltese derived originally from Phoenician and Arabic, with the addition of some words adapted from English and Italian.

263 **Maltese linguistic surveys.**
Joseph Aquilina.   Msida, Valletta: Malta University Press, 1976. 216p.

This work, in three parts, is composed of sixteen lectures which were delivered at international conferences. Part one covers linguistic cross currents, comparative Maltese and Arabic idioms, Maltese Christian words, the Berber element in Maltese and a survey of dialect. Part two deals with toponymy; and part three contains a study of 'nicknames' and surnames, compares Maltese and Arabic proverbs, and studies Maltese folklore.

264 **Simplified method to learn the Arabic language.**
Mohammed Sobhi Billo.   Valletta: Interprint, 1980. 152p.

An interesting work which shows the link between Maltese and Arabic.

265 **Maltese: how to read and speak it, phonetic pronunciation throughout.**
Paul Bugeja.   Valletta: A. C. Aquilina, 1974. 165p.

A primer which sets out the basics of learning the Maltese language.

266 **A historical review of the Maltese language.**
A. Cremona.   *Teacher's Magazine*, vol. 2, nos. 4, 6, 8 (1944); vol. 3, nos, 2, 4, 6-10 (1945), 28p.

The introduction of the study of Maltese into all state schools and the standardization of Maltese spelling, provided the stimulus for this series of articles, which together form a comprehensive history of the Maltese language. Cremona's study covers the origin and development of language and literature, systems for writing Maltese and the standardization of spelling. It will be of special interest to students of Maltese literature.

267 **Contemporary journalistic Maltese: an analytical and comparative study.**
Edward Fenech.   Leiden, Netherlands: Brill, 1978. 251p. bibliog.

This is the first comprehensive study of journalistic Maltese, which is a newer and less standardized form than the literary language. Fenech compares the two forms and concludes that journalistic Maltese is more 'daring' in accepting words and forms from the spoken and at times the colloquial language, and is more liable to be influenced by foreign languages.

268 **History of the Maltese language in local education.**
David Marshall.   Msida, Valletta: Malta University Press, 1971.
128p. bibliog.
This work traces the history and development of the teaching of the Maltese
language in schools, colleges and the university in Malta. It describes the way in
which Maltese became the official language, as well as the national language of
the islands.

269 **What is the Maltese language?**
Lewis F. Mizzi.   Valletta: Progress Press, 1923. 75p.
This short volume was written in order to promote the author's view that the
Maltese language is declining in use. Mizzi also puts forward two other theories:
namely that the development of Maltese is similar to that of modern Persian; and
that many Maltese words have been incorporated into the Italian language.

270 **A grammar of the Maltese language with chrestomathy and
vocabulary.**
E. F. Sutcliffe.   Valletta: Progress Press, 1960. 284p.
This useful study is one of the surprisingly few Maltese grammars to be published.

Dictionaries

271 **A comparative dictionary of Maltese proverbs.**
Joseph Aquilina.   Valletta: Giov. Muscat for the Royal
University, 1972. 694p. bibliog.
A collection of 4,630 proverbs, from both written and oral sources, and arranged
under 45 headings. The volume covers: epigrams; riddles and rigmaroles; puns;
the structure of proverbs; rhythm and rhyme; apophthegms; the links between
proverbs and folk verse; and much more. The study of proverbs can lead to a
greater understanding of a people's psychology, and often throws light on still
existing or abandoned beliefs, superstitions and customs, from which one can
piece together the whole social fabric of a country. Indexes of etymology, subject-
matter and the chief word of a proverb are provided.

272 **Kalepin, English-Maltese dictionary.**
E. D. Busuttil.   Valletta: Giov. Muscat, 1976. 542p.
The name Kalepin was given to the illustrious Italian lexicographer Ambrogio
Calepino, who was born in Bergamo in 1435 and died in 1511. This is one of the
surprisingly few dictionaries in English and Maltese.

273 **Dezionario Portatile delle lingue, Maltese, Italiana, Inglese.**
Da F. Vella.   Livorno, Italy: [s.n.], 1843. 167p.
One of the first English-Maltese dictionaries.

Religion

274   **The Church of St. John in Valletta 1578-1978.**
Edited by Father John Azzopardi.   Valletta: Progress Press, 1978.
116p.

This volume was written for the exhibition to commemorate the fourth centenary
of the consecration of the Church of St. John. It contains the exhibition
catalogue, as well as three articles on the works of art in St. John's, and a study of
the painter Michelangelo da Caravaggio, whose masterpiece 'The beheading of
St. John' is in the church's oratory.

275   **Saints and fireworks: religion and politics in rural Malta.**
Jeremy Boissevain.   London: Athlone Press, 1969. 162p. bibliog.

This valuable work provides an analysis of secular and religious politics in Malta
in the 1960s. It focuses on the importance of the cult of saints, which resulted in
conflict as the various political factions supported different saints, and there was
bitter rivalry between them. The volume also studies the clash between the
Church and the Labour clubs in the villages, highlighting the difficult role of the
parish priest, who was often caught between the two opposing groups.
Appendixes cover the Labour Party's election manifesto, festa and Band Club
Partiti.

276   **Church and State in Malta 1800-1850.**
Monsignor Arthur Bonnici.   Valletta: Giov. Muscat, 1958. 30p.

A brief study of the abolition of ecclesiastical immunities, Church-State relations,
and the freedom of the press, in the first half of the 19th century in Malta.

Religion

277 History of the Church in Malta.
Monsignor Arthur Bonnici. Valletta: Empire Press-Catholic Institute, 1967-68. 2 vols.

Volume one of this accurate, unbiased history, covers the period from AD60, the year that Christianity was brought to the islands, to 1530. Volume two studies the Church in Malta between 1530 and 1800. A third volume has been published (Zabbar, Malta: Veritas Press, 1975), and covers the period 1800 to 1975. Contents include the following; the attainment by the Maltese diocese of independence from the Metropolitan See of Palermo, the creation of the diocese of Gozo, the formation of the Maltese Episcopal Conference, and the spiritual and intellectual formation of the clergy.

278 Our Lady of Mellieha (Malta).
Raphael Bonnici Cali. Valletta: Progress Press, 1952. 51p. 2 maps. bibliog.,

This study of the Sanctuary of Our Lady of Mellieha, places it against the background of the general history of Malta and of the Church. It pays particular attention to its traditional apostolic foundation, and to the theory that its icon may have been brought to Malta by St. Luke.

279 The Church of our Lady of Victory: the first building in Valletta.
R. Bonnici Cali. Valletta: Information Department, 1966. 24p. bibliog.

A brief study of the Church of our Lady of Victory, which was completed in 1567 to commemorate the Great Siege victory.

280 Paul the traveller.
Ernle Bradford. London: Allen Lane, 1974. 256p. 2 maps.

A straightforward detailed account of Paul's journeys, of interest to both the layman and specialist. Paul's stay in Malta is covered on p. 223-30.

281 Catholic life in Malta AD60-1960.
Floriana, Malta: Catholic Institute, 1963. 52p.

This booklet was written to mark the 19th centenary of the introduction of Christianity to Malta. It provides a short summary of the Church's history on the islands.

282 Charisma of the primitive Franciscan fraternity.
Philip Cutajar. Valletta: Char Vin Press, 1983. 120p.

An historical study of the spiritual power, which was given to the Franciscans by God.

283 **The hand of John the Baptist.**
Victor F. Denaro. *Revue de L'Ordre Souverain Militaire de Malte*, no. 1, (1958), p. 33-38.
The venerated right hand of John the Baptist was brought to Malta by the Knights Hospitaller after the fall of Rhodes, and went with the Knights in 1798 to Russia. It disappeared in Yugoslavia during the Second World War.

284 **More about the hand of John the Baptist.**
Victor F. Denaro. *Scientia*, vol. 25, no. 3 (1959), p. 97-103.
This article asks whether science may be able to determine if the relic of the hand of St. John the Baptist is authentic.

285 **Relations between Church and State.**
A. Depasquale. Msida, Valletta: Malta University Press, 1974. [not paginated].
An in-depth analysis of church-state relations in general, with specific reference to Malta. It focuses on the issue of how much political power the church should have.

286 **Exposition of the Malta question with documents.**
Vatican City: Poliglot Press, 1930. 159p.
The Vatican's account of the conflict which arose between the Roman Catholic Church and the Maltese government in the 1920s. The government opposed the dominant role of the Church in Maltese affairs, and rebelled against the influence of Italy as a whole, including the wide-spread use of the Italian language in Malta. A papal delegate visited Malta in 1930, in an attempt to bring the Maltese into line, but he had little success. Throughout the 1930s, the Maltese church, led by strong cardinals, became increasingly independent of Rome.

287 **The making of Archbishop Gonzi.**
Dominic Fenech. Valletta: Union Press, 1976. 50p. bibliog.
An account of the appointment of Archbishop Gonzi in 1943. The British saw him as a threat to their position and made every effort to prevent his appointment. Yet despite this opposition, Gonzi went on to become one of Malta's most influential archbishops.

288 **Financial administration of the diocese church of Malta, August 1970.**
Valletta: Diocese Church of Malta, 1971. 70p.
This report discussed the need for a reorganization of the financial administration of the Church of Malta. It concluded that a more simplified system was needed, with centralized, professional management of property and investment.

Religion

289 **Brief historical notes on some smaller churches in Valletta.**
Michael Galea.   Zabbar, Malta: Veritas Press, 1972. 49p. bibliog.

This illustrated volume was based on a Maltese television series entitled 'Wirt Artna' (Malta's heritage). It covers the origins and history of the following churches: St. Lucia, St. Barbara, Our Lady of Liesse, St. Catherine, Our Lady of Pilar, St. James and St. Roque.

290 **Fabrizio Sceberras Testaferrata, a Maltese cardinal.**
Michael Galea.   *Scientia*, vol. 37, no. 3 (1974), p. 103-18; no. 4 (1974), p. 167-85.

A study of the distinguished Maltese cardinal, Fabrizio Sceberras Testaferrata (1758-1843), who in addition to his religious duties, was also well-known for his philanthropic work among the poorer sections of the community.

291 **The life and times of Vicenzo Labini, Bishop of Malta.**
Michael Galea.   Valletta: Vexillina Printing Press, 1980. 76p. bibliog.

A brief biography of Vincenzo Labini, the last foreign bishop of Malta. His episcopacy lasted from 1780 to 1807.

292 **Zabbar Museum guide.**
Mill Kappillan dun Gius. Zarb.   Rome: Grafiche IGAP, 1955. 40p.

A well-illustratd guide to the treasures of the Zabbar Museum, a church museum annexed to the Zabbar Sanctuary.

293 **A Maltese medal of 1679.**
Sir George Hill.   *Numismatic Chronicle*, 5th Series vol. 18, (1938), 5p.

Discusses the medal commemorating the laying of the foundation stone of the Choir attached to the Cathedral of Malta.

294 **Regular and secular clergy in Malta: cooperation or infighting in a Mediterranean Catholic regime?**
Adrianus Koster.   Amsterdam: Institute of Cultural Anthropology, Free University, 1983. 26p. bibliog.

An academic treatise on the relationship between the secular and the regular clergy in Malta.

295 **Malta: Church-State Labour, documents recording negotiations between the Vatican authorities and the Labour Party 1964-1966.**
Edited by Dom Mintoff.   Valletta: Freedom Press, 1966. 115p.

This work is divided into four main sections which cover: the period immediately preceeding the 1962 general election in Malta; the aftermath of the election; negotiations with the Vatican authorities; and the 1966 general election.

296 **The quarrel of the Malta Labour Party with the Church in Malta.**
Valletta: Special Diocesan Commission, 1966. 53p.

This booklet was produced in response to a pamphlet by Dom Mintoff, entitled
Malta – Church, State, Labour (q.v.), which was critical of the Church in Malta.
The Vatican did not consent to the publication of the documents contained in this
publication.

297 **The Church of St. John in Valletta: its history, architecture and
monuments, with a brief history of the Order of St. John from its
inception to the present day.**
Hannibal P. Scicluna, foreword by Sir Harry C. Luke.   Rome:
Casa M. Danesi, 1955. 344p. bibliog.

A very detailed and well-researched study of St. John's Church, with over 350
plates and a comprehensive glossary.

298 **From lordship to stewardship: religion and social change in Malta.**
Mario Vassallo.   The Hague: Mouton, 1979. 272p. bibliog.
(Religion and Society Series, no. 15).

For centuries, the Roman Catholic Church was the focus of national identity in
Malta, and was almost a surrogate form of political expression and nationalism.
Vassallo claims that, since the 1960s, the Church has been losing that function and
hence it has become less powerful and important. He studies the Church's
reaction to social change, paying particular attention to structural differentiation,
both in Maltese society and within the Church itself. The volume emphasizes the
incipient pattern of secularization on the islands.

299 **St. Paul, Christ's envoy to Malta. AD60-1960.**
Loreto Zammit.   Valletta: Giov. Muscat, 1960. 31p.

A booklet written for the celebrations of the 19th centenary of the shipwreck of
St. Paul, which led to the conversion of the Maltese to Christianity. The last three
chapters cover Paul's shipwreck and his stay on Malta.

300 **The presentation, examination and nomination of the bishops of
Malta in the 17th and 18th centuries.**
Antonio Zammit Gabarretta.   PhD thesis, University of Malta,
1961. 100p.

During the period under discussion, twelve bishops were nominated in Malta.

Politics

301 Voices and echoes: tales from colonial women.
Joan Alexander.   London: Quartet, 1983. 223p. bibliog.

Chapter sixteen of this volume (p. 180-95), provides an outline of the career of Mabel Strickland, daughter of the former prime minister of Malta, Sir Gerald Strickland.

302 Malta and the end of the empire.
Dennis Austin.   London: Cass, 1971. 144p. bibliog.

An account of the events leading up to Malta's independence. Austin attaches great importance to the proposition made in 1955, that Malta should be fully integrated into the United Kingdom. He sees this as 'a remarkable proposal which ran contrary to the general movement of colonial policy at the time'. The work is divided up into three chapters entitled: 'L'Angleterre d'outre-mer;' 'The 1956 referendum'; and 'Separation'.

303 Malta's road to independence.
Edith Dobie.   Norman, Oklahoma: University of Oklahoma Press, 1967. 286p. bibliog.

This volume studies the events which preceded Malta's independence, and the many problems which were connected with it. Hostility towards Britain grew as some political leaders in Malta presented Britain as a tyrant that must be forced to make concessions. Many Maltese politicians saw the attainment of power as an end in itself and did not plan how they would use it. The question of how much influence the Roman Catholic Church should have in Maltese politics also caused many difficulties. Finally, in 1964, a form of government was agreed upon, which provided independence within the Commonwealth and a curb on the power of the Church.

304 **Party politics in a fortress colony: the Maltese experience.**
Henry Frendo. Valletta: Midsea Books, 1979. 243p. bibliog.
Originally written as an Oxford University D. Phil. thesis, this is a pioneering work of Maltese historiography. It discusses the interaction of society and politics in colonial Malta, and emphasizes the island's difficulty in finding a national identity. The author examines constitutional change and political conflict within the country and questions whether a deeper sense of what is meant by being Maltese would prevent political clashes in the future.

305 **Is Malta burning?**
Michael Frendo. Valletta: Nationalist Party, 1981. 73p.
This booklet is an attack on the Labour government of Malta which, the author claims, has consistently attempted to destroy democracy in the country. It emphasizes the Nationalist Party's determination to revitalize democratic institutions. A useful glossary is provided.

306 **A meeting at the crossroads of history in Malta: Malta's attempt to become a part of the United Kingdom.**
Michael de Giorgio. Malta: BSc dissertation, University of Bristol, 1979. 43p. bibliog.
A study of the proposition made at the 1955 Round Table Conference in London, that Malta should be integrated into the United Kingdom. De Giorgio demonstrates that there was a historical precedent for the plan. He then goes on to analyse why Mintoff, as head of the Malta Labour Party administration, welcomed the proposal, and why some other groups in Malta were opposed to it.

307 **Malta's new premier – as critics see him.**
John Hatherley. *Contemporary Review*, vol. 246, no. 1433 (1985), p. 304-06.
This short article attempts to predict what sort of leader Malta's new prime minister, Carmello Mifsud Bonnici, will prove to be. It is expected he will pursue a more rigidly left-wing policy than his predecessor, Dom Mintoff; some people are even suspicious that Bonnici favours a one-party state. Much of the article is written from the viewpoint of Fenech Adami, the leader of the opposition in Malta, who believes that the Labour Party will be defeated at the 1986 election. The reasons given for this are the Labour Party's continued conflict with the Church, Malta's economic problems, and the belief that some of the vote that was for Mintoff personally will henceforth be denied to the Labour Party.

308 **Labour Manifesto: towards a greater well-being.**
Valletta: Information Division, 1981. 35p.
All aspects of Labour Party policy are covered in this 1981 manifesto.

309 **Report on his mission to Malta, Cyprus and Gibraltar 1948.**
Sir Harry Luke. London: Stephen Austin, 1948. 18p.
Part one (p.2-6) covers the author's visit to Malta.

310 **A memorandum on the dominion status of Malta.**
Fortunato P. Mizzi. *Studia*, (1964), 12p.
After the 1932 elections, a group of Maltese came to London, to seek the granting of dominion status for Malta. This reprint of the original document which the group presented provides a useful insight into Maltese political history.

311 **The Nationalist Party: 100 eventful years, a history of a Maltese political party. Part 1: mass meetings.**
Compiled by the Nationalist Party Office. Pieta, Malta: Nationalist Party, 1981. 12p.
A photographic account of the party at meetings and rallies.

312 **The acceptance of proportional representation in Malta.**
J. H. Proctor. *Parliamentary Affairs*, vol. 33, no. 3 (1980), p. 308-21.
Discusses the introduction and gradual acceptance of a proportionally-based parliamentary system in Malta between 1921 and 1976.

313 **Report by the Electoral Commission on the review of electoral boundaries 1970.**
Valletta: Central Office of Statistics, 1970. 15p. map.
An official report setting out in detail the need for changes in the electoral boundaries of Malta, in order to make the size of the constituencies more equal.

314 **The royal visit to Malta, November 1967.**
Valletta: Allied Malta Newspapers, 1967. 29p.
A pictorial account of the only official royal visit to Malta since the country was granted independence from Britain in 1964.

315 **Too early for Freedom: the background to the independence of Malta 1964.**
Dennis Sammut. Valletta: Private publication, 1984. 99p.
This is an interesting, illustrated and clearly written account of the background to Malta's independence, which analyses the attitudes and conduct of both the British and Maltese governments. It also provides a brief outline of Maltese society in the early 1960s, covering the conflict between the Church and the Labour Party and the economic hardship resulting from the mass dismissals of workers from the British bases and the naval dockyards.

316 **A colonial inheritance.**
Edward L. Zammit. Msida, Valletta: Malta University Press, 1984. 123p.
A concise study of work, power and the class structure in Malta, which also makes some references to the labour movement on the island.

Law and the Constitution

317 Constitution of the Republic of Malta.
Valletta: Department of Information, 1975. 102p.
Under this constitution, Malta became a republic within the Commonwealth on 13 December 1974.

318 The constitutional court issue in Malta. Il-kwistjoni dwar il-qorti kostitwzzjonali f'Malta.
Valletta: Camera Degli Avvocati, 1976. 64p.
This bilingual report provides a summary of the memo of April 1970, which dealt with the question of whether the office of Vice President amongst the judges, should be retained or abolished. It also contains the correspondence between the International Commission of Jurists and Malta's prime minister, and an extract from *The Review* of June 1974.

319 An assessment of the law relating to agricultural leases.
Paul Coppini.   Msida, Valletta: Malta University Press, 1979. 224p.
A study of the rules which govern agricultural leases under the Civil Code of Malta. It covers: the special rules which apply to rural tenements yielding fruit (the Metayer system); the 1941 and 1943 emergency regulations; and the 1967 act, which regulated the reletting of agricultural land.

320 The law on commercial partnerships in Malta.
F. Cremona.   Msida, Valletta: Malta University Press, 1975. 158p.
A legalistic detailed analysis of commercial partnerships in Malta, detailing their origin and development, kinds of partnership, their juridical character, limited

liability company, debentures, accounts, audit and annual return, the winding up of partnerships, and concluding comments on their viability.

321 **An outline of the constitutional development of Malta under British rule.**
J. J. Cremona.   Msida, Valletta: Malta University Press, 1963. 131p.
This work refers to the constitutions of 1831, 1835, 1849, 1887, 1903, 1921, 1936, 1939, 1947, 1959 and 1961 in Malta. A section is included on where to find the constitutional instruments and a selection of documents of constitutional interest is also provided.

322 **Human rights documentation in Malta.**
J. J. Cremona.   Msida, Valletta: University Press, 1966. 66p.
A report based on an international colloquy about the European Convention on Human Rights, held in Vienna in 1965. At the meeting, the member states of the Council of Europe demonstrated the ways in which they were trying to protect human rights and fundamental freedoms. Malta contributed seven documents which illustrated the development of human rights on the island.

323 **Governmental liability in Malta.**
Wallace Ph. Gulia.   Msida, Valletta: Malta University Press, 1974. 260p.
Written in English, Italian and Maltese, this work is a very useful textbook of Maltese administrative law. It consists of tables of cases and laws and regulations.

324 **Malta constabulary: consolidated report on the working of the police department for the years 1961-1967.**
Valletta: Department of Information, 1969. 121p.
A general account of all aspects of the work of the island's police force from 1961 to 1967.

325 **The Malta Constitution 1947.**
Valletta: Department of Information, 1947. 40p.
Under this constitution, Malta was granted a measure of self-government, while remaining under British rule. In 1961, this constitution was replaced by the *Malta (Constitution) Order in Council*, under which the island became known as 'the State of Malta.'

326 **Malta Independence Conference, 1963.**
London: HM Stationery Office, 1963. Cmnd. 2121. 148p.
This volume includes: a list of the people who took part in the conference; the chairman's report; an account of the amendments sought by the Malta Labour Party; the opinions of the Christian Workers' Party, the Democratic Nationalist Party and the Progressive Constitutional Party on the draft constitution; the co-citizenship proposal made by the Christian Workers' Party; and the interdepen-

dence proposal of the Progressive Constitutional Party. There are also seven annexes which reproduce the opening statements of Duncan Sandys, Dr. Borg Olivier, Dom Mintoff, Dr. Ganado, Mr. Pellegrini, and Mabel Strickland, and also provide an account of the Nationalist Party's amended draft independence constitution.

327 Malta Independence Constitution.
London: HM Stationery Office, 1964. Cmnd. 2406. 55p.

An official report describing the constitution of the state of Malta, and discussing citizenship, rights and freedoms, parliament, the executive, the judiciary, finance and public service.

328 Malta Review. Special Issue Malta Independence 21 September 1964.
Valletta: Department of Information, 1964. 35p.

The contents include: a profile of the prime minister; a study of the Independence Act; an historical outline of Malta; an account of constitutional development since 1800; details of general elections on the island; and a consideration of the commemorative stamp issue.

329 Malta Round Table Conference, 1955: report.
London: HM Stationery Office, 1955. Cmnd. 9657. 38p.

This detailed report examined the various views for and against Malta's becoming independent.

330 Malta statement of policy on constitutional reform.
London: HM Stationery Office, 1947. Cmd. 7014. 11p.

This report, which was presented by the Colonial Secretary, outlines Malta's constitution and the amendments to it, and also covers: security on the islands; the second chamber; the franchise; judges; the police force; reservation of bills; the legislative assembly; and the language issue.

331 Maltese constitutional and economic issues 1955-59.
Valletta: Progress Press, 1959. 143p.

A record of the Progressive Constitutional Party's official documents on constitutional and economic matters. The documents outline what were considered to be the prerequisites for any future constitution at this time. The volume covers: the London Conference; the Round Table Conferences; the request for representative government; and the PCP and five year plans on the island.

332 The making and unmaking of a Maltese Chief Justice.
Arthur Mercieca.   Valletta: Giov. Muscat, 1969. 379p.

An autobiography, illustrated by photographs, which pays a great deal of attention to Maltese politics, in particular, the granting of independence. The work also contains a useful summary of its fifty-eight chapters. It should be noted that because of his opposition to the Maltese government Mercieca was made to suffer isolation in his own house.

333   **The European Community: a comparative study with English and Maltese company law.**
J. Micallef.   Rotterdam, Netherlands: University Press, 1975. 765p. bibliog.
An academic work describing the evolution and character of economic and financial interests in relation to company law.

334   **Company secretarial practice in Malta.**
M. L. Petrocochino.   Valletta: Progress Press, 1967. 50p.
This short volume studies the Commercial Partnerships Ordinance in Malta and provides an account of company secretarial practice on the island.

335   **Aspects of Maltese law for bankers.**
Philip Farrugia Randon. Valletta: Institute of Bankers, 1983. 256p.
This textbook covers various aspects of Maltese law which are particularly useful to the Maltese banker. Chapters on 'Obligations' and 'Joint and several obligations' are included. This excellent reference book includes an interesting list of Maltese case law decided by eminent jurists on matters relating to banking practice.

336   **Report of the Malta Constitutional Commission, 1960. February, 1961.**
London: HM Stationery Office, 1961. Cmnd. 1261. 75p.
This report strongly supported the restoration of internal self-government in Malta. The constitution had been suspended in 1958 after the resignation of the Maltese government.

337   **Reports on the Working of Government Departments.**
Valletta: Department of Information, annual.

Military Affairs

338 **Civil defence in Malta (1951-1972): an historical sketch.**
E. H. W. Borg. *Armed Forces of Malta Journal*, no. 27 (1977), p. 9-13, 16.

A discussion of the role of civil defence in Malta and its effect on the economy and politics of the island.

339 **The history of Fort St. Angelo.**
H. G. Bowerman. Valletta: Progress Press, 1947. 53p.

This fort was an important stronghold of the Knights of Malta during the Great Siege (1565). During the Second World War it was the Royal Navy's headquarters, and survived repeated bombings. The fort is located at Vittoriosa, and commands an excellent view of the Grand Harbour.

340 **Historical records of the Maltese corps of the British Army.**
A. G. Chesney. London: William Clowes, 1897. 210p.

A unique study of the records of the Maltese corps from 1815 (all earlier material having been lost). It contains brief sketches of all the regiments, and appendixes which cover establishments and rates of pay of the Royal Malta Artillery, the Regiment of Militia and those Maltese who have served in the British Army.

341 **The cross and the ensign: a naval history of Malta 1798-1979.**
Peter Elliott. Cambridge, England: Patrick Stephens, 1980. 217p. bibliog.

This volume surveys Malta's naval history from 1798 to 1978. During most of this period, Malta was under British rule and the author traces the ways in which the history of the two nations was linked.

342 **Crusader castles.**
Robin Fedden, John Thomson. Beirut: Khayat's College Book Cooperative, 1957. 127p. map. bibliog.
Specific reference is made to castles in Malta, in this history of the military architecture of the Crusades.

343 **The *Royal Oak* courts martial.**
Leslie Gardiner. Edinburgh; London: William Blackwood, 1965. 258p.
A study of an incident which arose out of the British Government refusing to increase naval estimates and expenditure quotas in 1928. The Captain and some of the officers of the battleship *Royal Oak* refused to sail from Malta under Admiral Collard and were court-martialled and carried as passengers to Gibraltar. Many blamed her sinking in 1939 at the hands of a U-boat at Scapa Flow on the nebulous influence of the affair of 1928, but this has been dispelled by recent German accounts.

344 **History of the Royal Malta Artillery abridged for use in regimental schools.**
Valletta: Criterion Press, 1944. 40p.
A short history of the artillery compiled by a committee of RMA officers with additional notes by G. B. Harker. The volume also contains: an outline of Maltese history; a summary of European history since 1789; and a date chart.

345 **Fortress: architecture and military history in Malta.**
Quentin Hughes. London: Lund Humphries, 1969. 284p. 2 maps.
This account of Malta's architecture and military history is illustrated with reproductions of photographs taken by the author. Hughes stresses the unique character and history of the island.

346 **Britain in the Mediterranean and the defence of her naval stations.**
Quentin Hughes. Liverpool, England: Penpaled Books, 1981. 235p. bibliog. illus.
An account of the way in which Great Britain acquired, maintained and defended her naval stations, which includes many references to Malta. The volume covers the 19th and 20th centuries, with particular emphasis on the 19th century.

347 **Malta 1813-1914: a study in constitutional and strategic development.**
Hilda I. Lee. Valletta: Progress Press, 1972. 292p. map. bibliog.
An evaluation of the strategic importance of Malta, and an assessment of Britain's role in the Mediterranean during this period.

348   **Sea power in the Mediterranean: a history from the seventeenth
       century to the present day.**
       S. W. C. Pack, foreword by Admiral Sir J. Hamilton.   London:
       Arthur Barker, 1971. 260p. map. bibliog.

There are many references to Malta in this very informative illustrated study of
the influence of sea power on Europe.

349   **Sir Alexander Ball: the father of the Maltese.**
       J. W. Damer Powell.   *Blue Peter*, vol. 15, no. 156 (March 1935),
       p. 106-15.

An illustrated account of the part played by naval officer Alexander Ball in
Britain's capture of Valletta from the French in 1800.

350   **History of the Royal Malta Artillery. Volume I (1800-1939).**
       A. Samut-Tagliaferro.   Hamrun, Malta: Lux Press, 1976. 496p. 2
       maps.

This history of the Royal Malta Artillery shows how the role and status of a
country's military forces reflects the political philosophy and economic state of the
government in power.

Foreign Relations

351 **Agreement between the Government of the United Kingdom and the Government of Malta with respect to the Use of Military Facilities in Malta, London 26 March 1972 Treaty Series no. 136.**
London: HM Stationery Office, 1972. 44p.
The official account of the agreement between Malta and the UK on the use of military facilities in Malta. It provides a detailed coverage of the nine articles and the annex to the agreement.

352 **Agreement on Mutual Defence and Assistance between the Government of the United Kingdom of Great Britain and Northern Ireland and the Government of Malta (with related Exchanges of Letters).**
Malta 21 September 1964 Cmd. 3110. map. London: HM Stationery Office, 1966. 34p.

353 **Anglo-Maltese relations.**
London: Central Office of Information, 1971. 8p.
A brief history for general use describing Malta's constitutional development; its attainment of independence; the reorientation of the economy after independence; the defence agreement; Malta and NATO; British financial assistance; the rundown of British forces in Malta; the Anglo-Maltese Joint Mission; the dockyard; and the Anglo-Maltese Financial Agreement.

354 **Britain, Europe – and some Malta: Britain's political chastity.**
Dennis Austin. *Round Table*, vol. 240 (1970), p. 394-404.
A discussion of the effect which Britain's membership of the European Economic Community would be likely to have on the Commonwealth. At this time the

author suggested that on the evidence of Britain's relations with Malta between 1955 and 1964, 'the English are the least prepared psychologically "to enter Europe", if, by that, is meant sharing their autonomy with others.'

355 **Early relations between Malta and the United States of America.**
Paul Cassar.   Valletta: Midsea Books, 1976. 129p. bibliog.
A study of relations between Malta and the USA from 1790 to 1850. During the last decade of the 18th century, the USA began to use Malta as a supply station for its navy; as a place of shelter from the Barbary corsairs; and as a depot for their trade, especially tobacco. In return for this, the Knights of St. John anticipated the grant of some land in the US, but this never materialized.

356 **Cultural Agreement between the Government of Malta and the Government of the Libyan Arab Republic. Tripoli, 5 October, 1972.**
Valletta: Department of Information, 1972. 7p. (Treaty Series no. 142).
A detailed account of this controversial agreement, signed by the Prime Minister of Malta, Dom Mintoff, and the Libyan leader Colonel Qaddafi.

357 **The political economy of Malta: the economics of Mr. Mintoff's independence.**
John Dowdall.   *Round Table*, vol. 248 (1972), p. 465-73.
Discusses the impact of Mintoff's government on Malta's international relations and the country's potential economic development in the 1970s. It analyses the problems of Malta's economic growth, and studies the island's progress away from dependence on British military expenditure. The author argues that Mintoff's aggressive assertion of independence involved policy decisions that would ultimately limit his freedom of action.

358 **Malta: NATO and neutrality.**
Mario Felice.   Valletta: Council of the Malta Atlantic Association, 1971. 64p.
This volume was an attempt to promote the NATO cause. The author infers that the formula by which Malta's relations with NATO were governed had much room for improvement.

359 **Growing Soviet interests in Malta.**
London: Foreign and Commonwealth Office, 1982. 4p. (Background Briefs, no. 302.)
A report on the Soviet Union's increasing military and trade links with Malta.

360 **Malta's increased relations with neighbouring countries.**
A. J. Leaver.   In: *Malta Yearbook 1969*, p. 346-50.
A detailed appraisal of the island's foreign and inter-imperial role.

361 **Malta Treaty Series 1-100.**
Valletta: Department of Information, 1964-68.

A compilation of 100 treaties concerned with: mutual defence and assistance; financial assistance; the dockyard: the military; international rights and obligations; technical assistance; trade; migration; visa abolition; travel between countries; agreements with the EEC; investment guaranty; the continental shelf; road traffic; cultural agreements; drug prevention and slave traffic.

362 **Mediterranean maverick: Malta's uncertain future.**
Joseph V. Micallef. *Round Table*, vol. 275 (1979), p. 238-251.

This article presented the view that Malta's foreign policy in the 1970s, under Prime Minister Dom Mintoff, was uncertain because of Mintoff's unrealistic view of his country's strategic importance to both eastern and western powers.

363 **Neutrality Agreement: Malta-Italy 1980.**
Valletta: Ministry of Foreign Affairs, 1980. 46p.

The text of the agreement in English, Maltese and Italian. In 1981, the Ministry of Foreign Affairs also published *Neutrality Agreement: Malta-USSR*.

364 **NOW Malta.**
Valletta: Department of Information. 1965.

This illustrated work, published under the above composite title, consists of the following pamphlets linking Malta with international organizations: *Malta and the Council of Europe.* (June, 31p.); *Malta and the Commonwealth Prime Ministers' Conference.* (Aug. 32p.); and *Malta and the UN.* (Oct. 59p.)

365 **Official documents about the Malta Libyan dispute on the dividing line of the Continental Shelf. 8 September 1980.**
Valletta: Government Printing Press, 1980. 61p.

This booklet, written in both English and Maltese, contains the official correspondence between the governments of Malta and Libya over oil exploration.

366 **Peace in the Mediterranean: Malta's contribution.**
Valletta: Ministry of Foreign Affairs, 1984. 111p. map.

Following the departure of all foreign military forces from the island on 31 March, 1979, Malta assumed a status of neutrality based on the principal of non-alignment. A declaration of neutrality pronounced in the Maltese Parliament on 14 May 1981 has received recognition from twenty-one nations, the Non-Aligned Movement, the Commonwealth and the Conference on Security and Cooperation in Europe. This work is in three parts covering major policy statements; initiatives in the Conference on Security and Cooperation in Europe; and other initiatives.

367 **Malta's foreign policy after Mintoff.**
Godfrey Pirotta. *Political Quarterly*, vol. 56, no. 2 (1985), p. 182-86.

A clear and concise article analysing Malta's foreign policy in the 1980s. A comparison is offered between Dom Mintoff's policy and that of the current prime minister, Mifsud Bonnici. The author describes the current policy as a 'new look' in relation to Britain, the European Economic Community and NATO. The article also considers Malta's possible foreign policy in the future.

368 **Malta's permanent neutrality.**
Natalino Ronzitti. In: *Italian Yearbook of International Law*, vol. 5 (1980-81), p. 171-201.

This article asks whether Malta should be a neutral state, and questions whether or not it actually is neutral, as it claims to be.

369 **To the highest bidder: Malta, Britain and NATO.**
W. Howard Wriggins. *Round Table*, vol. 258 (1975), p. 167-85.

The author describes: the diplomatic negotiations between Great Britain and Malta in 1971 concerning rental payments for the naval base; the sources of Maltese bargaining power; Malta's role in the Cold War and particularly in NATO defences; and the country's success in using its geopolitical position. In the end a compromise agreement was reached between Britain and Malta, whereby rent for the naval base would be paid by Britain, while Malta would also receive aid from Italy and from the North Atlantic Treaty Organization.

Economy

370 **Malta – a developing economy.**
Maurice Abela. Valletta: Central Office of Statistics, 1963. 45p.

The author provides an account of the Maltese economy of the early 1960s and of the problems arising from its previous over-dependence on its value as a military base. Although the Maltese economy seems to have much in common with that of other countries of the European periphery, closer examination reveals dissimilarities which are even more striking than the resemblances. The author examines Malta's economic institutions, recent economic trends, the role of agriculture, changes in occupational structure, the demographic problem and the development plan.

371 **The economic problems of Malta: an interim report.**
Thomas Balogh, Dudley Seers. Valletta: Government Printing Office, 1955. 44p.

This report suggested improvements in Malta's economy, indicated the amount of aid expected from Great Britain, and stated what economic measures should be taken.

372 **Malta's first Five Year Development Plan 1959-1964.**
B. W. Blouet. *Geography*, vol. 34 (1964), p. 73-75.

An account of the first five year development plan which concentrated on the development of industry in Malta, particularly in the Valletta area.

373 **Malta: background for development.**
Howard Bowen-Jones. Durham, England: Durham University, Department of Geography, 1962. 362p.

An analytical account of Malta's socio-geographic and economic problems. The author stressed the need for Malta to develop its agriculture and industry after becoming independent of Britain.

374 A century of progress, 1848-1948.
Valletta: Chamber of Commerce, 1950. 68p.

An illustrated study of the important part which the Chamber of Commerce has played in Malta's history. It also discusses Malta's economic problems in the late 1940s.

375 Commonwealth development and its financing 10: Malta.
London: HM Stationery Office, 1966. 62p. 27 tables. bibliog.

A report on Malta's economy in the 1960s divided into three sections which cover: sources and use of funds; progress in the main sectors; and investment funds.

376 The politics of economic development: the Maltese experience.
James Craig. Manchester, England: Manchester University Press, 1983. 24p. (Manchester Papers in Development, no. 8.)

This monograph studies the development of Malta's economy since the island became independent in 1964.

377 The economic situation of Malta.
Kenneth Dallas. Valletta: Union Press, 1963. 52p.

A report to the General Workers' Union of Malta covering Malta's industrial potential; employment; the service industries; the dockyard; emigration; and foreign aid.

378 Focus on aspects of the Maltese economy, a critique of techniques used by M. M. Metwally in *Structure and performance of the Maltese economy.*
E. P. Delia. Valletta: Midsea Books, 1978. 71p.

These papers are a contribution to Maltese econometrics. Each paper evaluates a particular technique, or conclusion and puts forward suggestions for future research. The papers are entitled 'Multipliers for tourism,' 'Personal tax function' and the 'Single equation model.'

379 Economic and Social Studies.
Edited by E. P. Delia, E. J. Scicluna, E. L. Zammit. Msida, Malta: Faculty of Managerial Studies, University of Malta, 1983- . annual.

In the first issue of this journal there are articles by: E. L. Zammit 'Alienation, anomie and traditional powerlessness'; Edward Scicluna 'The measurement of public enterprise and productive efficiency, a suggested framework; and Godfrey A. Pirotta 'The Growth of trade unions under British colonialism: a comparative study'.

380 Overtaxed? A comment on the Maltese experience.
E. P. Delia. *Economic and Social Studies*, no. 1, 1983.

This article is critical of the high level of taxation in Malta over the past two decades, under both the Labour and Nationalist governments.

77

381 **Unemployment: internal and external factors.**
E. P. Delia.   Msida, Valletta: Malta University Press, 1983. 24p.

An assessment of the theory that Malta's unemployment problem is largely the
result of a world recession. It analyses Malta's exports and economic growth in
the 1970s and early 1980s.

382 **Development Plan for Malta, 1973-80.**
Valletta: Office of Prime Minister, October 1974. 206p. map.

A report supplemented with tables and charts, detailing Malta's economic
achievements and objectives. It outlines the 1973-80 Development Plan, and
analyses its social, economic and environmental implications.

383 **Economic Survey.**
Valletta: Economic Division, Office of the Prime Minister, August,
1981. 23p.

The fortunes of the Maltese economy are naturally linked to developments in the
world economy. The level of economic activity in the Maltese islands depends
both on the ability to export goods and services and on the importation, on
favourable terms, of capital equipment, industrial supplies and consumer goods.

384 **The future. Series of talks over the Redifusion System about the
future of Malta, broadcast between 29 October and 28 November,
1958.**
Valletta: Central Office of Information. 1958. 64p.

Written in English and Maltese, this brief work covers Malta's employment
prospects, docks and other activities in the late 1950s.

385 **Into the eighties: options for the economy.**
Valletta: Chamber of Commerce, 1979. 35p.

Malta's economy is no longer dependent on revenue from foreign military bases,
but the island has yet to reach its objective of viability, based on self-generating
economic growth. This booklet discusses Malta's economic problems in relation to
its resources and infrastructure, and studies the growth sectors of industry,
agriculture and tourism.

386 **Joint Mission for Malta. (Report 18 July, 1967).**
Valletta: Department of Information, 1967. 70p.

The task of this joint British-Maltese mission was to see how Malta's industrial
base could be strengthened and additional jobs created. Its report deals with
tourism, agriculture, the docks, manufacturing industry, construction, and the
training and placement of workers on the island.

387 **Joint Steering Committee for Malta. Second Progress Report January 1969 to September 1970.**
Valletta: Government Printing Press, 1970. 24p.

This Committee was concerned with the implementation of the recommendations of the report of the *Joint Mission for Malta* (q.v.) Its central thesis was that it would be possible to mobilize Malta's economic capacity on a scale sufficient to produce 15,000 new jobs by 1972.

388 **Malta builds an independent economy: new industries replace defence.**
Russell King. *Geographical Magazine*, vol. 50, no. 6 (March 1978), p. 373-80. map.

Malta's population thrived for 150 years by exploiting the natural resources of the island's fine harbour. However, the Soviet and US fleets are now banned, and the British services left in 1979. The author reports on the island's economic structure as the then prime minister, Dom Mintoff, continued his policy of 'Maltanization' to help the people become more self-sufficient. The new economy of Malta is being built on the tripod of manufacturing industries, marine services and tourism, but this tripod is still too shaky to bring the goal of economic development sharply into focus.

389 **Malta: guidelines for progress, Development Plan 1981-85.**
Valletta: Economic Division of the Office of Prime Minister, 1981. 240p.

A work discussing: Malta's economic framework; the objectives of monetary policy; the public sector programme; transport policies for air and sea travel; water; sewerage; and telephones.

390 **Structure and performance of the Maltese economy.**
M. M. Metwally. Valletta: A. C. Aquilina, 1977. 169p.

This study of the Maltese economy will be useful to the student, the researcher and the general reader. Malta's climate, harbour and low labour costs are all advantages to its economy, while it has the disadvantage of lacking deposits of coal, natural gas and petroleum.

391 **Unemployment in Malta, 1956-1971.**
Robin G. Milne. *Journal of Development Studies*, vol. 12, no. 4 (1976), p. 383-95.

This article examines the variables involved in unemployment in Malta between 1956 and 1971. It argues that lack of demand and rising labour costs were the main causes of unemployment.

392 **Malta's struggle for survival.**
Dom Mintoff. Hamrun, Malta: Lux Press, 1949. 83p.

This volume outlines the early political and economic views of Dom Mintoff, who was Prime Minister of Malta from 1971 to 1984. In this early work, Mintoff attempts to find a solution to his country's economic problems of the 1940s.

393 **Proposed association of Malta with the EEC. A report presented to the House of Representatives by the Minister of Commonwealth and Foreign Affairs, 19 October, 1970.**
Valletta: Department of Information, 1970. 93p.

394 **Quarterly Economic Review of Tunisia and Malta.**
London: Economist Intelligence Unit, 1968. quarterly.

Until 1984, this publication was entitled *Quarterly Economic Review of Libya, Tunisia and Malta*. It contains charts, market prices and statistics. There is also an annual supplement to this review which contains items about, and analyses of, the Maltese economy and the country's political life.

395 **A review of the economic situation in Malta.**
Valletta: Nationalist Party, 1982, 73p. 9 tables.

A survey of the cost of living in Malta, unemployment, exports and tourism, which was undertaken primarily to propagandize the Nationalist cause. The party contrasts their time in office in the 1960s, with the Mintoff administration since 1971, which they describe as a 'crisis unchecked'. The report ends with an analysis of the Nationalist alternative.

396 **The way to economic recovery: private sector's proposals.**
Valletta: Confederation of Private Enterprise, 1984. 72p.

The work centres on the continuous process of economic development as a means of achieving an increase in personal welfare, social well-being and a country's wealth. The Confederation maintains that concern must be given to the identification of the principles and means, which would lead to future economic cohesion and development. The study encapsulates the private sector's views of the economy and society in Malta, and offers suggestions and proposals to produce an economic recovery and an improvement in the quality of life. The study is in two parts: part one provides a general background; and the second part is devoted to the private sector's view of the economy and future proposals in the short, medium and long terms.

397 **The Maltese Islands: economic problems and prospects for industrial developments.**
B. S. Young, *Geographical Review*, vol. 53, no. 2 (1963), p. 263-86. map.

A monograph concerning Malta's: economic structure; population growth; development plans; industrial patterns; local materials; water supply; power; labour; capital; markets; and new industry.

Finance and Banking

398 **Taxation with tears. Book 1.**
     Gontran L. Borg.   Msida, Valletta: Malta University Press, 1968.
     26p.
The text of a talk delivered by a tax attorney at the University of Malta, which
focuses on the assessment of income tax in Malta.

399 **Central Bank of Malta Act, 1967 and subsequent amendments 1983.**
     Valletta: Information Division, 1983. 43p.
A legal treatise on the creation of the Central Bank.

400 **Central Bank of Malta: Quarterly Review, December 1984.**
     Valletta: Central Bank of Malta, 1984. 64p.
This review is prepared and issued by the Research Division of the Central Bank
of Malta. The opinions expressed here do not necessarily reflect the official views
of the bank. Contents include a financial survey, budget estimates and statistical
tables covering assets and liabilities, commercial bank liquidity, liquid assets,
loans and advances, interest rates, government revenue and expenditure, the
direction of trade, and retail price indexes.

401 **Taxation: an evaluation.**
     E. P. Delia.   Msida, Valletta: Malta University Press, 1981. 84p.
An independent study commissioned by a number of business institutes and the
Maltese Chamber of Commerce. It claims that Malta's tax structure should be
altered in order to facilitate economic growth, by providing an incentive for
individual effort and achievement.

402 **Exchange Control Act, 1972.**
Valletta: Information Division, 1972. 21p.

A work analysing the operation of the Exchange Control Act in relation to Malta's economy and financial relations with other countries.

403 **The Malta Currency Board, 1949-1968.**
Joseph Licari. *Journal of the Faculty of Arts*, vol. 4, no. 1 (1969).
p. 1-19.

An historical account of the board which controlled the supply of Maltese currency.

Trade and Industry

404 The British Five Year Plan for Malta.
Thomas Balogh, foreword by Dom Mintoff. Valletta: Labour
Party, 1963. 22p.
An analysis of the plan, together with an exchange of correspondence on the visit
to Malta of the Secretary of State for the colonies in December 1959.

405 Industries in Gozo.
G. N. Cassar. In: *Malta Yearbook 1960*. p. 175-79.
A factual and comprehensive survey of the island's industries, and their role in
the Maltese economy.

406 The outcome of fiscal policy: an assessment.
E. P. Delia. Valleta: Il-Hajja Press, 1982. 47p.
A study commissioned by the Chamber of Commerce, the Federation of
Industries, the Hotels and Restaurants Association, the Employers Association
and the Real Estate Federation which pays particular attention to the effects of
fiscal policy on industry.

407 The Exporter.
Valletta: Penprint, 1979- . monthly.
A trade review, published in English by Malta's Ministry of Trade, with a
circulation of around 5,000.

408 Free port in Malta.
Msida, Valletta: Malta University Press, 1965. 32p.
This pamphlet is an early study of the possibility of a free port in Malta, which is
still under consideration in the 1980s, although as yet, it is still only a proposal.

The work contains the following three appendixes: 'Considerations affecting the creation of a free port in Malta' by F. K. Liebich; 'General scheme for a free port in Malta', by I. Laucht and I. Mavers; and 'Model tests of the port of Marsaxlokk', by I. Hensen *et al.*

409 The significance of the tourist industry to Malta: assessment and new direction.
John C. Grech. Valletta: Chamber of Commerce, 1982. 56p.

A booklet in five sections, describing the growth of the vitally important tourist industry in Malta, which covers its economic impact, its development, a proposed plan of action, and the national objectives of tourism. Appendixes itemize tourist arrivals and the geographical distribution of holiday accommodation. Grech provides a thorough survey of tourism, and offers the recommendation that it should be de-politicised and run by professionals.

410 An industrialisation study of the Maltese Islands. Phase 1 – macroeconomic study of the conditions of development of industry in Malta for the Malta Development Finance Corporation, Ltd., Valletta.
A. M. Hatt-Arnold, E. Fontela, C. Tavel. Geneva: Institut Battelle, 1964. 76p.

This volume studied: the conditions which it was considered would foster industrial development in Malta; attempts to improve industry; and the concept of an export corporation.

411 Industry and the EEC. Malta-EEC relations: a study on the implications for industry of full membership or possible alternative arrangements.
Valletta: Federation of Industries, 1981. 71p.

This report, with twenty-four tables, discusses Malta's economic structure and the possible implications for industry of full membership of the European Economic Community (EEC), or of an alternative arrangement with it.

412 Industry Today.
Floriana, Malta: 1977- . monthly.

The official journal of Malta's Federation of Industries.

413 Lloyd Maltese.
Hamrun, Malta: 1846- . weekly.

A register of shipping published in English and Maltese.

414 Malta, where investment pays.
Valletta: Malta Development Corporation, 1981. 32p.

An illustrated report propagandizing the Malta Development Corporation, which was set up by the Maltese Parliament in 1967. The Corporation was a national agency entrusted with the promotion of industrial activity on the island. By the end of 1979, over 200 aided firms were operating in the Maltese manufacturing sector.

415 **An industrial survey and plan for Malta.**
O. W. Roskill. Valletta: Trade Development Office, 1951. 121p.
This report examined plans to develop industry, including agriculture and fishing, in Malta. The author studied monopolies and tariffs, technical knowledge, services, the building industry, management methods and facilities for new industries.

416 **A time series analysis of Malta's monthly imports 1960-1980.**
Lino Sant. Msida, Valletta: Malta University Press, 1982. 41p.
A thorough analysis of Malta's monthly imports for the period under discussion.

417 **Certified opinion on the possibilities of a development of tourism in Malta.**
Jur Ulrich Seelinger. Valletta: [s.n.], 1963. 33p.
A report outlining the geography, history, political status and economy of the islands. There are detailed descriptions of the preconditions for tourism, its organization, its position in 1963, and the possibilities for future development.

418 **The development of industry in Malta.**
Lino Spiteri. Valletta: Chamber of Commerce, Federation of Malta Industries; Employers' Association, 1969. 84p.
An outline of the islands' industrial potential in the face of changes in the industrial structure, new types of industries and the run down of British naval bases. An appendix on industrial development, estimates and expenditure is included.

419 **The cotton textile industry in Malta.**
A. P. Vella. *Melita Historica*, vol. 4, (1966), p. 210-15.
A short history of the economic importance of Malta's cotton textile industry.

Agriculture

420 The farmer and rural society in Malta: a report to the Colonial Economic Research Committee Project.
Brian W. Beeley. Durham, England: Durham University Press, 1959. 186p. maps.

This report provided a detailed study of Maltese rural society, covering: the social structure of the villages and the evolution of settlements; seasonal farming; mechanization problems; farmers' cooperatives and unions; government subsidies, the Agricultural Advisory Services; the living standards of farmers; agricultural marketing; and the problem of official neglect of the younger generation in farming.

421 Cultivation and diseases of fruit trees in the Maltese Islands.
J. Borg. Valletta: Government Printing Press, 1922. 622p.

This volume describes the types of fruit trees which are grown in Malta, and the conditions which produce them, such as the geology of the islands, bedrock and soil, and the water obtained through irrigation. It also provides an extensive study of the cultivation of fruit trees, and discusses the diseases which can afflict them.

422 Report on the social aspects of Maltese agriculture.
Renato Cirillo. Msida, Valletta: Malta University Press, 1959. 120p.

This pioneering report is the result of intensive fieldwork carried out jointly by the Department of Geography at Durham University, and the Royal University of Malta. The report contains the original findings on the following subjects: changes in village life; farmers' perceptions of government; consumption patterns and the standard of living in some Maltese villages such as Mġarr, Zabbar, Zejtun, Zurrieq, Siġġiewi, Għarb and Zebbuġ; social investigation of farmers living in Zebbuġ, Nadur and Gxarb on Gozo; land tenure and fragmentation; expropriation of agricultural land; marketing of agricultural products; farmers' attitudes to cooperative societies; farming equipment; the loans and grant scheme; and the effect of the agricultural situation on emigration patterns.

423   **A study of the agriculture, marketing and rural society in the Maltese islands with special reference to Gozo.**
Muriel Hatter.   London: University of London, School of Oriental and African Studies, MA dissertation, 1977. 44p.
This agricultural and rural study includes: a detailed analysis of marketing and retail operations in Rabat in Gozo; a survey of shoppers in Rabat; a survey of shopping visits to Rabat by other Gozitan villagers; and a sociological description of Gozitan villages and village stores.

424   **Soils of Malta and Gozo.**
D. M. Lang.   London: HM Stationery Office, for Colonial Office Research Studies, no. 29, 1960. 112p. map. bibliog.
A study of the soil, its geological base, and its role in the development of agriculture. The work is supplemented by plates, plans and tables.

425   **Food production in Malta, G.C., during the 1942 siege.**
E. E. Skillman.   *Agriculture: Journal of the Ministry of Agriculture*, vol. 50 (1943-44), p. 481-87.
An article outlining the climate, food production, conditions of husbandry, potato harvest and vegetable production of Malta during the Second World War siege. It describes the main problems faced by farmers whose livestock was almost entirely dependent on imported feed.

Labour and Labour Relations

426 **Alternative industrial relations systems for Malta.**
Msida, Valletta: Malta University Press, 1971. 78p.
These papers cover the proceedings of a seminar held in the Economics Department of Malta University. The theme of the seminar was the interrelationship between workers, management and government.

427 **Industrial relations in Malta.**
Joseph Attard. Hamrun, Malta: Peg Publications, 1984. 194p.
The first part of this volume provides a history of industrial relations in Malta, including the effects of legislation and the origins and functions of trade unions. The second part focuses on the Industrial Relations Act of 1976, while part three provides an analysis of worker participation in industry. This is a valuable reference work, which takes a new look at industrial relations in Malta.

428 **Workers' participation in Malta, issues and opinions: report of research in four companies.**
Gerard Kester. Msida, Valletta: Malta University Press; The Hague: Institute of Social Sciences, 1974. 231p.
This volume, the result of surveys carried out in four companies, attempts to assess the viability of worker participation in Maltese industry. It studies the rights of management, workers' representation and ownership perceptions.

429 **Transition to workers' self-management: its dynamics in the decolonising economy of Malta.**
Gerard Kester. The Hague, Netherlands: Institute of Social Studies, 1980. 255p. bibliog. (Research Report Series no. 7)
This study concentrates on the search for policies and formats which would lead to workers' self-management in Malta. The author is sympathetic to the idea of the democratization of labour relations.

430 **The labour market and wage determination in Malta.**
Edward Clifford Koziara. Msida, Valletta: Malta University Press, 1975. 120p.
The purpose of this study is to examine the way in which wages are determined in Malta, and to analyse the characteristics of the Maltese labour market. As there was a lack of published material on the subject, recourse was made to interviews with union leaders, employers, scholars and government officials. The work also discusses the differences and similarities between the labour movements in Malta and other European countries. It will be valuable to both the student and the general reader.

Statistics

431 **Census of the Maltese Islands.**
Valletta: Government Printing Press and Progress Press, 1861- .
irregular.
The last census in Malta was in 1977, and it covered such topics as population
growth, nationality and occupations.

432 **Statistical Abstracts of the Maltese Islands.**
Valletta: Central Office of Statistics, ca. 1947- . annual.
This volume includes a wide range of data on, for example, industry, the
economy, demography and labour. Other useful publications by the Central
Office of Statistics include: quarterly and annual trade returns; annual vital
statistics; a quarterly digest of statistics; *National Accounts of the Maltese Islands*
(annual*); Balance of Payments* (annual); *Demographic Review of the Maltese
Islands* (annual); and annual statistics on education; shipping and aviation;
agriculture and industry.

433 **Statistical Yearbook.**
New York: United Nations, Statistical Office, 1948- . annual.
An up-to-date compilation of statistical information on all the member states of
the United Nations, including Malta. Subjects covered include the following:
education; housing; science and technology; agriculture; manufacturing; transport; communications; industrial production; unemployment figures; and tourism.

434 **Trade Statistics 1984.**
Valletta: Central Office of Statistics, 1984. 384p.
A statistical account of Malta's trade in the first six months of 1984. It describes
imports under broad economic categories; and provides comparative tables of
annual trade, imports and total exports, domestic exports and re-exports, as well
as statistical tables for the quarter and year to date. It also contains a glossary and
an index.

Environment and
Water Supply

435 The public gardens and groves of Malta and Gozo.
Joseph Borg.   Valletta: Men of Trees, 1979. 140p. bibliog.
This work, the first of its kind, was written in order to encourage an appreciation
of the natural beauty of Malta and Gozo.

436 The campaign against pollution of our environment.
A. J. Gera.   *Armed Forces of Malta Journal*, no. 16 (1973), p. 78-
79.
One of the first articles ever published on the subject of the threat of pollution to
Malta.

437 The water supply resources of Malta.
T. O. Morris.   Valletta: Government Printing Press, 1952. 125p.
map.
The need for an organized, municipal water supply in Malta has arisen in the last
four centuries, due to increased urbanization and a rapid growth in the
population. This study provides a critical appraisal of developments in water
supply between 1610 and 1945. It also covers the reorganization of the storage
and distribution of water, the present position of irrigation supplies, and the
prospects for deep boring.

438 The water supply of the Maltese Islands.
Themistocles Zammit.   Valletta: Government Printing Press,
1931. 54p. bibliog.
A brief history of the water supply of Malta, which demonstrates its importance
to successive governments.

Transport and Communications

439   **Malta: the story of Malta and her stamps.**
      James A. Mackay.   London: Philatelic Publishers, 1966. 96p.
A general, very readable work covering the philatelic history of Malta. It is divided into sections which cover early Malta, St. Paul in Malta, the Knights, modern Malta, Malta and the Second World War and the postal history of Malta. Some form of postal system existed in the latter years of the rule of the Knights, but no distinctive postal markings other than talismanic inscriptions of religious significance have been recorded during this period. One of the first acts of the British in Malta, therefore, was to establish a packet agency at Valletta to handle external mail. Appendixes include Anthony Trollope's report on the Malta Post Office, the Malta Study Circle, and an informative list of Malta's stamps.

440   **The Malta Railway.**
      B. L. Rigby.   London: Oakwood Press, 1970. 63p. 3 maps. bibliog.
The Malta railway was built in 1892, and it was hoped that it would revitalize the economy and create wealth. It was operative until 1931, when the competition of buses and coaches proved too powerful. The railway had the main part of its line in Valletta, but it also reached the more rural areas of the island.

441   **Ferry Malta. Il-Vapuri ta Ghawdex.**
      Graeme Somner.   Kendal, England: World Ship Society, 1982.
      42p. map.
This booklet describes the history of the ferry service between Malta and Gozo and the types of boats which were used.

442   **Franco-Maltese postal relations from their origins to 1870.**
      Henri Tristant.   Valletta: Emmanuel Said, 1983. 56p.
This pamphlet is an edited translation of the French original.

Social Conditions, Health and Welfare

443 **Medical history of Malta.**
Paul Cassar.   London: Wellcome Historical Medical Library,
1964. 586p. 2 maps.

A history of medicine in Malta from prehistoric times to the 20th century. The
author asserts that under the Order of St. John, medical organization in Malta
probably reached its peak. Maltese young men studied medicine, not only in the
medical school of Malta, but also in the universities of Italy, France and later
England. Thus, they brought back the high standards and latest advances of the
continental medical schools. This volume demonstrates how war and trade both
brought in their wake appalling epidemics of plague, cholera, leprosy and other
diseases. The work is divided into ten parts, which cover: the hospitals; medical
work under the Order of St. John; the pattern of disease in Malta; the
development of public health; communal health and welfare; nursing and
midwifery; the development from primitive belief to scientific thought; the 19th
century; and the impact of war. Another interesting work by Paul Cassar is *The
institutional treatment of the insane in Malta (up to the end of the 19th century)*. It
outlines the improvements which were made in the treatment of the insane, and
compares psychiatry in Malta with the rest of Europe.

444 **Landmarks in the development of forensic medicine in the Maltese
Islands.**
Paul Cassar.   Msida, Valletta: Malta University Press, 1974. 54p.
bibliog.

An academic paper prepared for a meeting of the International Academy of Legal
Medicine and Social Medicine. It studies: the Justinian legal enactments (ca.529-
564 AD), which regulated the practice of medicine, surgery and midwifery, and
represented the highest point in the development of forensic medicine in the
ancient world; the first known medical certificate to be issued in Malta in 1583;
and the establishment of a Medical Council in Malta in 1959, which was the first
time that ethical rules governed the practice of medicine in Malta.

445 **Sir Themistocles Zammit and the controversy on the goat's role in the transmission of brucellosis Mediterranean fever 1909-1916.**
Paul Cassar.   Valletta: Information Department, 1981. 31p. bibliog.

Brucellosis was a major cause of sickness and disability both among the civilian population and the British garrison in Malta during the 19th and early 20th centuries. This illustrated booklet outlines the controversy surrounding Zammit's discovery in 1905 that infected goat's milk was a cause of brucellosis in humans.

446 **The British naval hospitals at Malta with particular reference to Bighi, and the adjacent Church of SS o Salvatore.**
J. F. Darmanin.   *Archivum Melitense*, vol. 10, no. 4 (1939), p. 34.

An outline history of the hospitals, supplemented by letters.

447 **Changes in the epidemiological pattern of disease in the Maltese Islands.**
F. F. Fenech, R. Ellul Micallef, M. Vassallo.   In: *Contributions to Mediterranean studies*. Edited by M. Vassalo.   Msida, Valletta: Malta University Press, 1977, p. 221-31.

A fascinating historical and geographical account of disease in the islands.

448 **Leprosy in Malta.**
Joseph Galea, Edgar Bonnici.   *Leprosy Review*, vol. 28, no. 4 (1957), p. 139-46. bibliog.

In Malta, the first cases of leprosy, one of the oldest diseases in the world, were brought by the Phoenicians. In 1659, a commission was appointed by the Grand Master to care for the sufferers of leprosy.

449 **Sociological sketches, Malta 1972.**
Gunnar Hägglund.   Valletta: Union Press, 1972. 47p.

A collection of eight articles by a Swedish sociologist. The first one outlines the science of sociology and assesses its present position and possible future in Malta. Other subjects include: coverage of trade and industrial relations in *The Times of Malta* and *Malta News*; mobility in a Valletta slum; Maltese broadcasting; and a comparison of the penal systems in Sweden and Malta. The volume was written in the hope of starting a public debate about the potential of sociology in Malta.

450 **Malta 1972-1980: an evaluation of social policy.**
P. R. Kaim-Caudle.   Durham, England: University Centre for Middle Eastern and Islamic Studies, 1981. 28p. Occasional Papers Series, no. 10.)

A monograph discussing the political and economic evolution of Maltese social policy from 1972 to 1980.

451 **The history of the School of Anatomy in Malta.**
J. L. Pace. .Msida, Valletta: Malta University Press, 1971. 120p.
A study of the School of Anatomy in Malta, illustrated with many high quality plates.

452 **Youth and development in Malta: report of the Commonwealth Youth Seminar in Valletta, April, 1972.**
London: Commonwealth Secretariat, 1972. 180p.
Part one of this report covers the education, training and employment of the youth of Malta; part two deals with youth programmes and youth in the service of the community; and part three surveys juvenile delinquency, youth employment and pupil guidance. The report concludes that Maltese society has good intentions towards its youth, but that these are frustrated by a lack of commuication between generations. The result is that young people feel isolated and this reinforces their general sense of insecurity.

453 **Collected papers on diabetes in Malta and its cardiovascular complications and some other cardiological topics.**
Joseph V. Zammit Maempel. Msida, Valletta: Malta University Press, 1979. 93p.
This is a collection of some of the author's most important research papers. Malta is a suitable place in which to conduct epidemiological research, as it is a small island with a stable population, served by only one large general hospital.

454 **Diabetes in Malta: a pilot survey.**
J. V. Zammit Maempel. *The Lancet*, (1965), p. 1,197-200.
A survey of the reasons for the high incidence of diabetes mellitus in the Maltese islands. The article contains eight tables and two letters.

Education

455 The destruction of the University of Malta.
Dennis Austin. *Minerva*, vol. 19, no. 1 (1981), p. 126-34.

A detailed history, with documents, of the university between 1971 and 1980. It studies the events and viewpoints surrounding the change in status of the University of Malta, which lost its autonomy, putatively, in order to reorient the university to local needs.

456 Education: Journal of the Faculty of Education
Msida, Valletta: University of Malta, 1982-. quarterly.

This journal was established by the University of Malta in order to provide a forum for educational topics which are specifically relevant to Malta, but which may not have an international bearing. The first issue contained articles on the difference between the sexes in achievement in science subjects; the normative foundation of lifelong education; and the value of discussion in the teaching of English as a foreign language.

457 Hyphen.
1977- . quarterly.

Hyphen is the journal of the Upper Secondary School in Valletta, and its aim is to encourage the intellectual and moral development of the pupils. It contains articles in both English and Maltese.

458 The University of S. Maria Portus Salutis.
Andrew Vella, offprint from *Journal of Faculty of Arts*, vol. 2, no. 2 (1962), p. 164-80.

A study of the old and little-known Studium Generale which existed in Malta more than two centuries ago and which was founded by the Order of Friars Preachers.

459   **The University of Malta a bicentenary memorial.**
      Andrew P. Vella.   Valletta: Malta University Press, 1969. 165p.

An account of the first two hundred years of the University of Malta. It uses both published works and manuscript sources, and includes many footnotes and references in order to stimulate further research. The volume is illustrated with photographs, and contains nine appendixes, some of which are in Latin and Italian.

Literature

460   **Maltese meteorological and agricultural proverbs.**
Joseph Aquilina.   *Journal of Maltese Studies*, vol. 1. (1961), p. 1-80.

A list of proverbs arranged under the following headings: the sun, the moon and the stars; winds; clouds; lightning; thunder and rain; the sea; land cultivation, plants and fields; animals; the seasons; and the months of the year.

461   **A Maltese anthology.**
A. J. Arberry.   Oxford, England: Clarendon Press, 1960. 280p.

A series of extracts from Maltese literature covering proverbs, folk tales, popular songs, riddles, prose writings, and poetry. Maltese literature is a comparatively modern development. It has experimented with a wide variety of styles, but insularity of outlook has always been hard to overcome.

462   **Oleanders in the wind.**
Joseph Attard.   Valletta: Progress Press, 1976. 327p.

The story of a brilliant doctor who devotes himself to work among the simple folk on the island of Gozo, determined to improve their life. He wins the love and respect of all, only to find that his people could be swayed by misconceptions like . . . oleanders in the wind.

463   **The ghosts of Malta.**
Joseph Attard.   Valletta: Gulf Publishing, 1983. 179p.

An exciting historical novel of the occult.

464 **Malta: the new poetry: an anthology of modern Maltese verse.**
Edited by M. Azzopardi. Valletta: Klabb Kotba Maltin, 1971.
187p.
An English-language anthology of Maltese poetry.

465 **A wheel in Orion.**
Hella Jean Bartolo. Zabbar, Malta: Veritas Press, 1973. 30p.
A series of poems arranged under the following headings: 'Bellatrix', 'Betel-geuse', 'Theta Orionis' and 'Rigel', some of which are illustrated.

466 **The Malta connection: a thriller set in Malta.**
Hella Jean Bartolo. Valletta: Progress Press, 1976. 105p. map.
A suspense story involving the murder of a British resident in Malta. Scotland Yard, Middle East secret agents and midnight meetings at the seat of the Maltese government are just some of the ingredients of this action-packed novel.

467 **Malta caper.**
Hella Jean Bartolo. Valletta: Progress Press, 1981. 210p.
A novel of intrigue with a Maltese background.

468 **Tinsel and Gold.**
Joseph Bartolo. Valletta: Progress Press, 1983. 78p.
A volume of poetry divided into two parts. The 'Tinsel' section comprises poems written during the author's schooldays, when the world seemed to be full of promise. 'Gold' is a selection of later poems, which demonstrate the author's greater maturity and his often bitter experience of life.

469 **A poetic galaxy.**
Mario F. Bezzina (et al.). Valletta: Poet's Association, 1983. 48p.
A collection of contemporary Maltese poems by the following writers: Mario F. Bezzina, Amante Buontempo, Godwin Ellul, Alice Grech, Carmel Magro, Alfred Massa and V. M. Pellegrini.

470 **The lamplighter.**
Anton Buttigieg. Isle of Skye, Scotland: Aquila, 1977. 90p.
The majority of the poems in this volume are translated from the Maltese. They display a kindly irony and a deep feeling for the countryside.

471 **Tony the sailor's son.**
Anton Buttigieg, translated by William Driscoll. London: Onyx Press, 1983. 150p.
Anton Buttigieg, former president of Malta, affectionately recalls characters and incidents from his childhood in a series of delightful vignettes. In spite of the hardship and grinding poverty of pre-war life on Gozo, the people described here had a zest for life and enjoyed the simplest of pleasures to the full.

Literature

472 **Island of the seven hills.**
Zoe Cass. London: Cassell, 1975. 272p.
The island of Gozo, is the delightful setting of this novel of romance and suspense. Beautifully evoked in all its moods, the island and its people are as much a part of the story as the expatriates who bring crime and violence to its age-old tranquility.

473 **An alley in Malta.**
Guże Chetcuti, translated from Maltese by Maud Ruston. Zabbar, Malta: Veritas Press, 1976. 134p.
A novel illustrated with many drawings recounting with perception and amusement the lives of the neighbours of Stefan, who on his father's death moves with his mother and younger brother and sister to an alley in Valletta. The novel describes the neighbours' quarrels and their love affairs and Stefan's own great love which is hindered by the fierce jealousy of his mother and the sordid occupation of Romilda.

474 **Vassalli and his times: a biography.**
A. Cremona, translated by May Butcher. Valletta: Giov. Muscat, 1940. 228p.
An illustrated biography of Vassalli, who is considered to be the father of Maltese literature.

475 **In the eye of the sun.**
Francis Ebejer. London: Macdonald, 1969. 158p.
The powerful story of the disintegration of a brilliant student, through a psychotic return to his peasant origins and traumatic past. A novel of intense drama, grandeur and ingenuity which is set in Malta.

476 **The bicultural situation in Malta.**
F. Ebejer. In: *Individual and Community in Commonwealth Literature.* Edited by D. Massa. Msida, Valletta: Malta University Press, 1979. p. 210-216.
A critical appraisal of Maltese literature and the current standing of literary criticism.

477 **Requiem for a Malta Fascist (or The interrogation).**
Francis Ebejer. Valletta: A. C. Aquilina, 1980. 243p.
This powerful novel describes love, lust and intrigue during the brutal Nazi siege of the Maltese islands. The majority of the events described in the novel are drawn from the author's recollections of the war. Ebejer provides a vivid impression of what it was like to grow up in Malta in those turbulent times. This is a political novel, which attempts to show that politics are a reflection of human passions.

478   **Leap of Malta dolphins.**
      Francis Ebejer.   New York: Vantage Press, 1982. 254p.
An historical novel with a Maltese background.

479   **The Siege of Malta.**
      S. Fowler Wright.   London: Tom Stacey, 1972. 728p.
A dramatic and romantic story of La Vallette, Grand Master of the Order of St.
John, and the girl whose bravery wins his love.

480   **Cross winds: an anthology of post-war Maltese poetry.**
      Compiled by Oliver Friggieri, edited by Konrad Hopkins, Ronald
      van Roekel.   Paisley, Scotland: Wilfion Books, 1979. 125p.
      bibliog.
An introductory essay by Friggieri, entitled 'In search of a national identity'
places post-war poetry in the context of Maltese literature as a whole. This
anthology, which includes work by twenty-one poets, contains a representative
selection of post-war poetry in Malta. It includes both romantic and modernist
poems, as well as some which attempt to integrate the two styles.

481   **New bearings in modern Maltese poetry.**
      Oliver Friggieri.   *Trends*, vol. 2, no. 4 (1979), p. 45-54.
A review of current developments, trends and ideas in Maltese poetry. *Trends* is
the literary magazine of Paisley College of Technology, in Paisley, Scotland.

482   **Fire at the opera house: a novel of Malta.**
      Guze' Galea translated into English by J. G. C. Beck.   Valletta:
      [s.n.], 1965. 126p.
An illustrated novel, based on the real-life event of a fire at the Malta Opera
House.

483   **Stories of the war.**
      Guze' Galea.   Valletta: Union Press, 1970. 100p.
This work is meant to convey an image of the people of Malta in their every day
life during the Second World War. It contains fourteen stories which all describe
an extraordinary circumstance, or a tragic event of the war.

484   **Top ten tales of Malta 1977.**
      Edited by V. Lewis.   Valletta: Midsea Books, 1977. 79p.
This volume is the result of a national annual competition for the short story of
the year. The stories are by Joseph Zammit, George Cassola, Joe Bonnici, J.
Parnis, Gorden Galea, Carmen Debono, Pamela Miller, Frans Blundell, Gerald
Nethercot and Frederick Barrey.

485 **The Maltese writer in exile.**
D. Massa.   In: *The Commonwealth writer overseas*. Edited by A.
Niven.   Brussels: Didier, 1976. p. 63-74.

An article analysing the role of Maltese authors in exile and the pressures and
freedoms which they face on being away from their homeland.

486 **The Kappillan of Malta.**
Nicholas Monsarrat.   London: Cassell, 1973. 576p.

This novel is a powerful evocation of the Second World War in Malta, which
focuses particularly on the years 1940 to 1942. It is based on the life and work of
the Kappillan Father Salvatore.

487 **A baroness of Malta: a romance of the early sixteenth century.**
J. A. de' Conti Sant-Manduca, translated from the Maltese of S.
Frendo de Mannarino, translated from the Maltese of S. Frendo de
Mannarino.   Hamrun, Malta: Lux Press, 1953. 161p.

This exciting story set in 16th-century Malta, demonstrates the author's great
knowledge and love of his country.

488 **Encyclopedia of literature.**
Edited by Joseph T. Shipley.   New York: Philosophical Library,
1946. vol. 2.

A survey of world literature. The section on Malta (p. 682-87) by Hannibal
Scicluna mentions the main Maltese literary figures and discusses the new trend
for Malta to look to Britain and America for literary inspiration instead of Italy.

489 **Maltese poets of the 20th century.**
G. Tonna-Barthet.   Valletta: Giov. Muscat, 1968. 443p.

A selection of the work of fifty Maltese poets, which includes poems in Maltese,
English, French, Italian and German. It contains examples of both the early and
the mature work of the poets and there is a short biography and a picture of each
of them.

490 **Drama in Malta (a personal flashback).**
H. E. C. Weldon.   Malta: The Author. 133p.

A novel of the Second World War, written by a member of the Malta gunners.

491 **Peter Caxaro's 'Cantilena': a poem in Medieval Maltese.**
G. Wettinger, M. Fsadni.   Hamrun, Malta: Lux Press, 1968. 52p.
endpaper. map.

An account of the earliest published poem in Maltese which is also the earliest
evidence of written Maltese. It was discovered in September 1966 and consists of
twenty lines divided into three sections of six, four and ten lines, with a short
introductory paragraph in Latin. The language it uses is very different to
contemporary Maltese.

The Arts

492 **Sacred art in Malta.**
Vincenzo Bonello, John Cauchi.   Floriana, Malta: Catholic
Institute, 1960. 142p.
An account of an exhibition of ancient and modern art held under the auspices of
the National Pauline Committee.

493 **Lyric opera in Malta 100 years ago.**
M. A. Borg.   Valletta: National Press, 1939. 70p.
This unusual publication describes the 1838-39 opera season in Malta. It covers all
aspects of Malta's Royal Opera House, including the company's repertoire, its
conductor, the prima donna and the basso cantate. There are five appendixes and
three pages in Maltese.

494 **Works of art in Malta: losses and survivals in the war.**
Compiled by Hugh Braun.   London: HM Stationery Office, 1946.
48p.
The report of a committee which was set up to investigate the damage caused to
works of art in Malta during the Second World War. The concentration of many
architecturally important buildings around the dockyard area, meant that many
were damaged by bombs, particularly between 1940 and 1943. There was little fire
damage as all of Malta's buildings were made from the island's limestone.

495 **Antonio Sciortino 1947.**
Helene Buhagiar.   Valletta: [s.n.], 1947. 30p.
A catalogue of an exhibition commemorating the work of a foremost Maltese
sculptor. Many of Sciortino's masterpieces were presented as a free gift to the
people of Malta, and can now be seen in the National Museum of Fine Arts in
Malta. Works include allegorical subjects, original plaster models, bronzes,
marbles and terracotta.

496 **The works of art in the churches of Malta and the Governor's Palace, Valletta.**
Giuseppe Calleja, translated and edited by G. N. Godwin. Valletta: Maltese Press, 1881. 203p.
A work written for lovers of the fine arts in general and particularly as a guide for English visitors. It aims at correcting inaccurate statements made by badly-informed sacristans and unintelligent guides.

497 **The Gozo story: a background to crafts from 2,000 BC to 2,000 AD.**
Marie Claridge, with drawings by Boz. Valletta: Progress Press, 1972. 48p. bibliog.
An account of the history of crafts in Gozo, which covers weaving, stonework, agriculture, fishing, pottery, lacework, knitting, crochet, embroidery and other practical arts. It is comprehensively illustrated with forty-three line drawings.

498 **Norbert Attard, artist in Malta: offset lithographs 1977-1983.**
Dominic Cutajar, foreword by Richard England. Valletta: Sapienza's, 1983. 52p.
A pioneering study of the lithographer.

499 **The Manoel Theatre.**
V. F. Denaro. *Melita Historica*, vol. 3, no. 1 (1960), p. 1-4.
The Manoel Theatre, based on the design of the Palermo Theatre, was built in 1732, and is still in use today.

500 **Drawings of Malta.**
Patrick Hamilton, introduction by Ernle Bradford. Valletta: Progress Press, 1970. 60p.
A collection of thirty-one drawings, which capture the essential quality of Malta.

501 **A handbook of Roman art: a survey of the visual arts of the Roman world.**
Edited by Martin Henig. Oxford, England: Phaidon, 1983.
This general work includes a useful article on Maltese sculpture, (p. 66-96), by Anthony Bonanno.

502 **Caravaggio's paintings in Malta: some notes.**
Jacob Hess. *Connoisseur*, (1958), p. 142-47.
A brief study of the paintings which Michelangelo da Caravaggio produced during his visit to Malta in 1607.

503   **Michelangelo Merisi da Caravaggio.**
      Paul de Majo.   Valletta: Department of Information, 1959. 35p.

This booklet provides an analysis of Caravaggio's work, in order to stimulate further interest in him in Malta. One of his masterpieces, 'The beheading of St. John' hangs in the oratory of St. John's Co-Cathedral In Valletta, and is widely accepted as being the finest painting in Malta.

504   **Antique Malta: 1842-1885. A topographical and historical catalogue of engravings and articles as depicted in the major English magazines of this eventful period.**
      Compiled by A. Nicolas, with a preface by J. Galea, A.
      Ganado.   Valletta: Progress Press, 1982. 114p.

A comprehensive catalogue of engravings, which, together with the original articles, present a mass of specialized information furnished by eye-witnesses of events, costume and character. The engravings include the foundation of the Royal Opera House, the proposed extension of the original dockyard, the Royal visitors to the island, the traditional parades, and some cartoons of curious characters now forgotten.

505   **Melchior Gafa Maltese sculptor of the baroque, further biographical notes.**
      Edward Sammut.   *Scientia*, vol. 23, (1957), p. 117-39.

A study in English and Italian of Melchior Gafa, one of Malta's most important sculptors.

506   **The Royal Malta Opera House: an historical sketch.**
      A. Samut-Tagliaferro reprints from *Sunday Times of Malta* Dec.
      1965 and Jan. 1966. 15p.

A brief history of the Royal Malta Opera House, which was burnt down twice in the 19th century and bombed in 1942.

507   **Gianni Vella, Maltese artist painter 1885-1917.**
      Aldo Vella, foreword by John Cremona.   Valletta: Progress
      Press, 1979. 128p.

Numerous colour and black-and-white reproductions of Gianni Vella's paintings dominate this study of his work. Vella, a countryman and a devout Christian, is best known for his paintings of nature.

Cuisine

508   Recipes from Malta: a guide to traditional Maltese cookery.
Anne Caruana Galijia, Helen Caruana Galijia.   Valletta: Progress
Press, 1972. 70p.

A work written in defence of Maltese cookery for which there has only been a
recent demand. It is the first volume to consist entirely of typically Maltese
recipes and is a useful introduction for both tourists and native Maltese.

509   Maltese cuisine.
Anton B. Dougall.   Valletta: Union Press, 1974. 52p.

The principal aim of this book is to introduce Maltese dishes to foreign visitors. It
enables the tourist to recreate Maltese dishes at home, and is also useful for
catering students and chefs who want to add some Maltese dishes to their menu.

510   Cooking the Maltese way.
Marie Vella.   Valletta: Cordina's 'Emporium' General Stores,
[n.d., ca. 1970], 64p.

This compilation of recipes was written in response to the demand for recipes of
Maltese dishes.

Folklore

511 **Holiday customs in Malta and sports, usages, ceremonies, omens, and superstitions of the Maltese people, and other useful material.**
E. D. Busuttil.   Valletta: Empire Press, 1964. 80p.
A welcome addition to the literature on the folklore of the islands. It describes the varied customs in an historical and factual way.

512 **An introduction to Maltese folklore.**
Joseph Cassar Pullicino, foreword by J. Aquilina.   Valletta: Allied Malta Newspapers, 1947. 47p.
This rather cursory work is an attempt to rectify the neglect of the scientific importance of Maltese folklore. The author brings together some ancient Maltese beliefs and customs, fearing that otherwise they will be lost for ever.

513 **Song and dance in Malta and Gozo.**
Joseph Cassar Pullicino.   *Journal of the English Folk Song and Dance Society*, (1961), p. 63-71.
Folk-music has a long tradition in Malta and is still popular today, although the influence of modern pop music has led to the disappearance of many songs. Folk-music has often been looked down on, and there has even been legislation to control the activities of folk singers. The Spanish guitar is by far the most popular musical instrument with the modern Maltese.

514 **Studies in Maltese folklore.**
Joseph Cassar Pullicino.   Msida, Valletta: Malta University Press, 1976. 279p.
A work written by one of the most scholarly authorities on this branch of ethnographic science. For many years Maltese folklore was an object of mere

curiosity, a collection of old wives' tales, but hardly the object of systematic analysis. However, this author has collected folktales, riddles, folk-songs and other specimens of folk-literature from Malta and Gozo, brought them together and studied them, not only in relation to one another, but also in relation to the folklore of other Mediterranean countries, especially Sicily and some countries of North Africa. Aspects of folk heritage throw light on ancestral habits and ways of life which often form the social fabric of past generations. An interesting feature of this book is the historical study of various customs and practices, some of which are still current.

515 **Maltese folk-tales.**
L. Galea, Margaret A. Murray. Valletta: Empire Press, 1932. 58p.
This collection of folk-tales was compiled by Manuele Magri with the help of Liza Galea and published in Maltese under the title *Xi jgheid il-Malte*. This English-language version contains notes which point out any differences from the original Maltese and provide background information on the folk-tales. It also includes a list of words known as the 'baby-language', which is a possible survival from a primitive language underlying the Semitic dialect.

516 **'Il Maltija', a Maltese national country dance for piano.**
H. M. Griffin. London: [s.n.], 1952. [not paginated]
A description of this unique dance which originated many centuries ago. It is considered to be the Maltese national dance.

517 **Maltese Folklore Review.**
Balzan, Malta: Maltese Folklore Review, 1962-73. irregular.
This journal contained articles in English and Italian on the social history, customs, traditions and folklore of Malta.

Architecture

518   **The Inquisitor's Palace Vittoriosa-Malta.**
John Camilleri.   Valletta: Privately published, ca.1970. 28p.
A description of the palace owned by the Inquisitor, who was an ecclesiastic appointed by the Pope to protect the Catholic faith and the Christian morals of the Maltese people.

519   **The architectural work of the Order of St. John of Jerusalem in Malta.**
Anne Joyce Cooke.   London: Privately published, 1931. 58p.
An illustrated survey of the architectural work of the Order of St. John, including an account of the materials they used and the most important buildings they constructed, most of which were in Valletta.

520   **The houses of Valletta.**
Victor F. Denaro.   Valletta: Progress Press, 1967. 129p. bibliog.
A collection of articles of architectural interest first published in the journal *Melita Historica*. The volume contains a plan of Valletta, a photographic survey of the town and a study of the streets of major historical interest.

521   **Heritage of an island, Malta.**
Michael Ellul.   Valletta: Government Printing Press, 1975. 83p.
A brief, yet comprehensive survey of Maltese architecture from prehistory to the end of the 19th century, which also includes a short section on painting and sculpture.

Architecture

522 **Walls of Malta.**
Richard England, foreword by A. C. Sewter. Valletta: MRSM, 1971. [not paginated.]
A study, based on photographs, which attempts to bring out the harmony between Malta's landscape and its architecture.

523 **Uncaged reflections (selected writings 1965-80).**
Richard England foreword by Peter Serracino Inglott. Valletta: MRSM, 1981. 175p.
A collection of writings by the well-known Maltese architect, Richard England. The subjects include architecture in Malta, a defence of the environment, art in Malta, appreciations, music and poetry.

524 **In search of silent spaces, quiescent dreams in borrowed time: a journey towards tranquillity, including the making of a garden for Myriam.**
Richard England. Valletta: MRSM, 1983. 96p.
A selection of poetry and comments on Maltese architecture.

525 **Sliema art nouveau architecture, 1928-1937.**
Renato la Ferla. Valletta: Progress Press for the Malta Chamber of Architects and Civil Engineers, 1969. 20p.
A brief work discussing the principal events and personalities of the art nouveau movement, and their effects on the development of architecture in Sliema which at this time was dominated by Italianate designs.

526 **Mdina: the silent city.**
J. Galea. Hamrun, Malta: Lux Press, 1948. 24p.
A guide emphasizing the architectural value of the city of Mdina including the Roman Villa, the main gate, the Connaught Hospital and the beautiful Baroque cathedral, built by Lorenzo Gafà.

527 **The work of architect Richard England in Malta. A research towards a contemporary regionalism, with introductory notes on the Maltese vernacular.**
Emile Henvaux. Brussels: Editions de la Librairie Encylopédie, 1969. 131p.
A lavishly-illustrated work, written in English and French. It covers the wide range of England's architecture, from hotels, villas and apartment blocks to churches and commercial and administrative buildings.

528   **The fortification of Malta by the Order of St. John, 1530-1798.**
Alison Hoppen.   Edinburgh: Scottish Academic Press, 1979.
215p. bibliog.
An extensively illustrated study of the fortifications built in Malta by the Order of
St. John. It contains an appendix on currency and measurements, and a glossary.

529   **The building of Malta during the period of the Knights of St. John
of Jerusalem 1530-1795.**
J. Quentin Hughes.   London: Alec Tiranti, 1956. 242p. map.
bibliog.
The author looks at Malta's architecture in the context of the Mediterranean as a
whole. The influences of France, Spain and Portugal are most apparent because
many grand masters of the Order of St. John were from these countries. Other
influences are explained by the fact that the knights also tried to maintain contact
with the rest of Europe. This is a very comprehensive study, with over 330
illustrations.

530   **An introduction to Maltese architecture.**
Extracts from *The Sunday Times of Malta* of 23 and 30 January, 6,
13, 20 and 27 February and 12 March, 1944. 24p.
These extracts form a short illustrated survey of Maltese architecture.

531   **Connections: the architecture of Richard England 1964-1984.**
Charles Knevitt, introduction by Dennis Sharp.   London: Lund
Humphries, 1983. 207p. bibliog.
A study of the work of Richard England, one of Malta's most important architects
of the 20th century. It discusses the influence of the Modern Movement on his
early work, contrasting this with his recent buildings, which display a fresh
interest in the minutiae of form. One of England's problems has always been that
the traditional Maltese way of building has restricted architectural development
on the island.

532   **The city of Valletta.**
E. R. Leopardi.   In: *Malta Yearbook*, 1967. Edited by Hilary A.
Clews.   Sliema, Malta: de la Salle Brothers. p. 316-22.
A study of the architectural history of Valletta.

533   **Malta's heritage in stone. Wirt Malta Fil-Gebel.**
**A collection of photographs compiled by the National Trust of Malta
(Din L-Art Ħelwa) to mark European Architectural Heritage Year
1975.**
Valletta: Midsea Books, 1978. 112p.
A photographic survey, depicting Malta's rich architectural heritage. Malta has
been invaded by both Western and Middle Eastern powers, who have all
introduced their own styles of architecture to the islands. This volume shows the

harmony between Malta's native architecture and that brought by the invaders. There is a wide range of temple architecture on the islands including the prehistoric megaliths of Skorba and Tarxien and, in towns such as Mdina and Valletta, important palaces and civic buildings. There are also some intriguing examples of trogloditic architecture. The captions to the photographs in this volume are in both English and Maltese, while the main text is in English only.

534 Re-representation, interpretation, imagination.
A. Mollicone.   Valletta: Aquilina, 1983. 69p.

A concise appraisal of architectural decoration and antiquities in Malta. This work is written in notebook style and is amply illustrated with plans and facsimiles.

535 Tumas Dingli 1591-1666.
Joseph A. Tonna.   Valletta: Chamber of Architects and Civil Engineers, 1966. 23p.

This study of Dingli's architecture provides a genuine appreciation of his work. Dingli's greatest contribution to architecture was his idea of order and cohesion in architectural planning.

536 Romano Carapecchia: studies in Maltese architecture I.
Joseph A. Tonna, Dennis de Lucca.   Msida, Valletta: Malta University Press, 1975. 41p.

A fascinating study of the 18th-century architect Romano Carapecchia, who became chief architect to the Order of St. John. Carapecchia designed St. Catherine's nunnery, the Palazzo di Litta, and the Vaini Palace, as well as the following churches: St. James, St. Catherine of Italy and St. Barbara.

537 The Roman villa in history.
Paul Xuereb.   Malta: Freedom Press, 1969. 32p.

There are many references to the Maltese Islands in this informative and readable study. Particular attention is given to the villas at Rabat and Mdina.

Numismatics

538 **The Malta Siege ingots of 1799.**
Victor F. Denaro. *Numismatic Circular* (London), Dec. 1956.
3p.

A description of the gold and silver ingots struck in Malta in 1799 by General Vaubois, who commanded the Napoleonic troops blockaded in Valletta.

539 **The Maltese obsidional coins of 1800.**
Victor F. Denaro. *Numismatic Chronicle*, 6th Series, vol. 18, (1958), p. 173-76.

A learned description of obsidional coins, which are coins struck in a beseiged city to supply immediate needs in the absence of sufficient regular coins. After the capture of Malta by the French in June 1798 gold and silver was seized in various churches and converted into 30-tari pieces.

540 **Dutch coins and Maltese countermarks.**
Victor F. Denaro. *Numismatic Chronicle*, 7th Series, vol. 3, (1963), p. 149-55.

The grand masters' economic policies were threatened by the arrival of Dutch coins, some of which were forged. The great influx of Dutch coins was largely due to the increase of Dutch commerce with the Levant, and the greater demand for Dutch currency.

541 **Maltese numismatics: a bibliography.**
Victor F. Denaro. *Scientia*, vol. 31, (1965), p. 1-36.

An introductory study, which will be of use to the student of Maltese numismatics and currency. The study is divided into ancient times; the Knights of Malta; the French occupation; and the period of British rule.

542   **The goldsmiths of Malta and their marks.**
Victor F. Denaro.   Florence, Italy: Leo S. Olschki, 1972. 241p.
bibliog.

In this study, the term goldsmiths is taken in its widest sense to include both the goldsmiths and silversmiths, most of whom produced works in both the precious metals. It discusses goldsmiths in the time of the Order of St. John, the French occupation and British rule. It deals with their work, church plate, domestic silver and marks on silver. Appendixes cover measures of weights, and tables of gold and silver standards. The work is richly illustrated by plates.

543   **The coinage of the Knights of Malta.**
Felice Restelli, Joseph C. Sammut.   Valletta: Emmanuel Said, 1977. 2 vols. bibliog. plates.

This valuable study provides a precise and detailed description of every known coin of the period. It is written in a straightforward style, making it suitable for the inexperienced collector as well as the professional numismatist. The authors have drawn on information which has only been made available this century and have also made good use of their personal collections. The various mottoes and subjects of the coins provide a fascinating insight into the history of the order. The volume also contains four appendixes which cover the monetary system, coinage tables, countermarked copper coins and grand masters of the order.

544   **Said Malta Coin, Banknote and Medal Catalogue, 1982.**
Emmanuel Said.   Valletta: Emmanuel Said, 1982. 103p.

The increasing interest in the coinage and paper currency of Malta prompted the compilation of this catalogue for collectors concerned with numismatics and or paper money. Some of Malta's modern coin issues and paper currency are extremely rare.

545   **Coins and medals of the Knights of Malta.**
H. Calleja Schembri.   London: Eyre & Spottiswoode, 1908. 262p.

The first description in English of Maltese numismatics. It is divided into three sections covering: coins struck between 1530 and 1572; coins from 1572 to 1798; and the medals struck by the Order of St. John between 1530 and 1798. A summary of the life of each grand master is included. An appendix provides a translation of official documents relating to the order and tables show the value of the coins in 1908.

Sports and Recreation

546 **A new approach to Maltese gardening.**
Joseph Buttigieg. Valletta: The Author, 1972. 144p.

This is a concise guide to the successful growing of vegetables, annuals, shrubs, roses, pot plants, climbers, fruit trees and ornamental trees. It provides a great deal of interesting information, and is the ideal volume for every keen gardener.

547 **Diving around the Maltese Islands.**
Harvey Fudge, Bob Harris. Valletta: Progress Press, 1975. 60p.
map.

A work written at a time of rapid growth in the sport of aqualung diving. Malta's stable weather conditions make it an ideal place for divers and many come to the island with no previous knowledge of its facilities for diving. In this volume, information concerning the hiring of equipment, local regulations regarding diving, availability of air, recompression facilities, and diving sites is gathered together for the first time.

548 **Rock climbing in Malta.**
J. D. Graham foreword by Maurice Dorman. Valletta: Royal Mountaineering Club, 1971. 103p.

This brief work comprehensively records the known and attempted climbs in Malta. It is in ten sections, with three appendixes providing information on the geology of Malta; on identifying climbs; and on climbing equipment required in Malta. There is also a good index of climbs.

549 The amateur gardener in Malta.

Joseph C. Mompalao de Piro.   Valletta: Progress Press, 1964.
72p.

Written by an amateur for the amateur, this volume outlines the basic principles of gardening. Useful appendixes provide a list of annuals, bulbs, corms and roots, vegetables, herbs and roses which are suitable for cultivation in Malta.

550 Walks and climbs in Malta.

Showell Styles.   Valletta: Progress Press, 1944. 79p.

This is a pocket guide to the Maltese coasts and countryside, written in wartime by an experienced mountaineer, stationed in Malta. The first part contains twelve routes for walks in the most beautiful parts of the island. The second part is for climbers and contains thirty rock climbs. A brief outline of the history, geology, archaeology and natural history of Malta is provided in this concise volume.

Newspapers and Periodicals

English Language Newspapers

551 The Bulletin.
　　Pieta, Malta: Independence Print, 1946- . weekly.
This paper, which supports the Nationalist Party, is similar in style and reporting to *The Times of Malta*.

552 The Democrat.
　　Pieta, Malta: Independence Print, 1975- . weekly.

553 The Sunday Times of Malta.
　　Valletta: Strickland House, 1922- . weekly.
A quality paper, which is considered to be one of the most authoritative in the islands. It is generally pro-British.

554 The Times of Malta.
　　Valletta: Strickland House, 1935- . daily.
This is the only English-language daily newspaper in Malta, and has a circulation of around 17,000. It is upmarket, informative, and generally pro-British.

555 Weekend Chronicle.
　　Valletta: Union Press, 1955- . weekly.
A paper reflecting the views of the General Workers' Union.

Maltese Language Newspapers

556 **Il-Ħajja.** (The Life.)
Valletta: Independence Print, 1970- . daily.
Written from a Catholic viewpoint.

557 **Il-Ħsieb.** (The Ideal.)
Valletta: 1952- . monthly.
A Labour Party paper, which is progressive in outlook.

558 **Leħen is-Sewwa.** (Voice of Truth.)
Floriana, Malta: Catholic Institute, 1928- . weekly.

559 **Il-Mument.** (The Moment.)
Pieta, Malta: Independence Print. weekly.
Presents the viewpoint of the Nationalist Party.

560 **L-Orizzont.** (The Horizon.)
Valletta: Union Press, 1962- . daily.
The chief mouthpiece of the General Workers' Union.

561 **In-Taghna.** (Ours.)
Pieta, Malta: Independence Print, 1970- . daily.
A Nationalist Party paper.

562 **It-Torca.** (The Torch.)
Valletta: Union Press, 1944- . weekly.
This Sunday paper expresses the views of the General Workers' Union.

Periodicals

563 **Heritage: an Encyclopedia of Maltese Culture and Civilization.**
Valletta: Midsea Books, 1977- . monthly.
This illustrated English-language periodical covers: Maltese history, including the history of architecture, politics, medicine, literature, and the church; archaeology; folklore; music; art; and the mass media.

564 **Journal of Maltese Studies.**
Msida, Valletta: Malta University Press, 1961- . irregular.
An academic journal providing a general coverage of Maltese history and culture. It contains articles in English, French and Italian.

118

565 **Malta Today.**
Valletta: Information Division, 1966- . bimonthly
Provides a general survey of Malta and is published in English with a circulation
of 3,500. It was formerly entitled *Malta Review.*

566 **Maltese Review: A Quarterly Review of Culture and Politics.**
1950- . quarterly.
This journal aims to bring together the best Maltese minds in all disciplines. It
strongly supported the aim of Maltese independence, which was achieved in 1964.

567 **Mediterranean Studies.**
Valletta: Midsea Books, 1978- . semi-annual.
This journal covers the history, culture and civilization of the Mediterranean
region, including Malta. It focuses in particular on contemporary affairs and
problems, such as the acculturation and erosion of Mediterranean characteristics;
pollution and exploitation of natural resources; trade and economic change; and
political tension and the effects of the presence of the superpowers.

568 **Scientia.**
Valletta: Scientia, 1935- . annual.
This scholarly journal, with articles in English and Italian, focuses particularly on
the history, theology and philosophy of Malta. It also provides some coverage of
folklore, art, medicine, educational and church history, law and natural sciences.

569 **Tomorrow.**
Valletta: 1982. monthly.
Tomorrow, a popular magazine, focuses mainly on contemporary Maltese affairs
and lifestyles. Its subject matter is varied and somewhat unusual. For example,
the contents of the first issue included cartoons and articles entitled: 'British
heritage'; 'The jobs women do'; 'Do Maltese enjoy sex?'; 'The recession and how
to beat it'; and 'My Mercedes is bigger than yours.'

Bibliographies

570 **Index historicus.**
Carmel Cuschieri.   Msida, Valletta: Malta University Press, 1979. 151p.
A classified index of articles in a select list of periodicals and collections of studies relating to Maltese history, which includes an author and an analytical index.

571 **A handlist of manuscripts in the British Isles relating to Malta.**
Gordon Donaldson.   Valletta: Government Printing Press, 1950.
85p. (Institute of Historical Research Publication, no. 7)
This volume was compiled for the Historical Archives of Malta Committee. It provides an accessible record of information which was previously very difficult to obtain. The entries, most of which are quotations from catalogues, are arranged topographically; that is, under the name of the town or county where they can be found.

572 **A bibliography of children's literature in Malta 1966-1976.**
Victor Fenech.   Valletta: Malta Library Association, 1976. 18p.
It is only over the last two decades that children's books have emerged as a distinct genre of Maltese literature. This bibliography is divided into six separate sections: reading in stages; narrative (original); narrative (translations and adaptations); bible stories; people and places; and poetry. Books are listed according to year of publication and authors are listed in alphabetical order.

573 **Malta and the Second World War.**
Joseph Galea.   *Melita Historica*, vol. 1, no. 1 (1952), p. 33-49.
The classification of this listing enables easy reference. Publications are arranged under four main headings: narrative; descriptive; political; and miscellaneous. These headings are further subdivided into: books; pamphlets; sections in books;

articles in periodicals; and press references. The period covered extends from 1939 to 1950. This is a very comprehensive list, which includes the many different perspectives on the war in Malta.

574 **Bibliography of the Great Siege of Malta 1565-1965.**
Joseph Galea. Mdina, Malta: Malta University Press, 1965. 135p.
An authoritative bibliography of all the books, articles and academic papers which have been written on the Siege of Malta.

575 **Melitensia: Books in Print.**
Valletta: Sapienza's, 1985. 55p.
An annual publication, covering books published in Malta and books published abroad which refer to Malta. It contains eleven specialized sections and a general section. Another work of interest to the bibliophile is *Directory of publishers, printers, book-designers and bookdealers* (Valletta: Library Association, 1981.)

576 **A handlist of writings on art in Malta.**
Edward Sammut. *Melita Historica*, vol. 4, no. 1 (1964), p. 34-52.
This work consists of a main list of writings about art in Malta, which is divided into historical periods; a list of general works; and a list of artists arranged in alphabetical order. In order to place Malta in the context of European art as a whole, Sammut also provides a short list of European art.

577 **Agriculture in the Maltese Islands.**
Norah Sammut. Msida, Valletta: Malta University Press, 1979. 76p.
An extremely comprehensive bibliography which contains 563 entries on Maltese agriculture. It covers: maps; treaties; reports; the land; climate; hydrology; water resources; crop production; horticulture; viticulture; animal husbandry; the dairy industry; economics, planning and development; education; cooperatives; afforestation and gardening; nutrition; farmers and rural settlements; and agricultural legislation and terminology. Sources have been collected from a wide variety of libraries.

578 **Royal University of Malta Library Melitensia Collection. List of periodical holdings.**
Anthony F. Sapienza, Mari Schinas. Msida, Valletta: Malta University Press, 1971. 17p.

579 **A checklist of Maltese periodicals and newspapers in the National Library of Malta (formerly Royal Malta Library) and University of Malta Library.**
Anthony F. Sapienza.   Msida, Valletta: Malta University Press, 1977. 37p.
This is not a definitive list of Maltese periodicals; nevertheless, it contains 1,222 entries and is an essential reference work for research workers in the field of Maltese studies.

580 **Bibljografija nazzjonali ta' Malta 1983.** (The national bibliography 1983.)
Edited by J. B. Scicluna, A. F. Sapienza, L. Sciberras, P. Xuereb.   Valletta: National Library of Malta, 1984. 41p.
The aim of this work is to list and describe every new work published in the Maltese Islands during 1983, and also to include everything written about Malta, by Maltese authors, but published abroad. It contains an index of authors, titles and series, as well as an index of subjects.

581 **A checklist of British official publications relating to Malta 1801-1950.**
D. H. Simpson.   *Melita Historica*, vol. 1, no. 3 (1954), p. 150-55.
A work which is of great value to researchers and specialists.

582 **A bibliography of Malta 1939-45: a revision and addition.**
J. R. Thackrah.   Ilkley, England: 1975. 15p.
The listing which will be of use to both the historian and the layman, covers primary and secondary sources of information on the Second World War in Malta. It includes 740 items, and is classified in order to facilitate easy reference.

583 **University of Malta publications 1983.**
Msida, Valletta: Malta University Press, 1983. 9p
A pamphlet providing details of the records of the Order of St. John of Jerusalem in the National Library of Malta, as well as publications by various authors, historical series, doctoral theses, textbooks, adult education series, faculty journals, and official publications.

584 **Economic and social history of Malta in the 19th century: a bibliography based on the holdings of the Royal University Library.**
Compiled by Paul Xuereb.   Msida, Valletta: Royal University of Malta Library, 1970. 20p.
This bibliography is suitable for both undergraduate and post-graduate students of Maltese economic history.

585　**Melitensia: a catalogue of printed books and articles in the Royal University of Malta Library referring to Malta.**
　　Paul Xuereb.　Msida, Valletta: Malta University Press, 1974. 76p.
This bibliography contains: works of a general, descriptive or historical nature; guidebooks; works containing accounts of Malta by visitors; biographies of prominent Maltese; and general works on Malta's geography, flora and fauna.

586　**Theses and dissertations submitted for the degrees of the Royal University of Malta.**
　　Paul Xuereb.　*Journal of Educational Affairs*, vol. 2, (1976), p. 72-86.
The items in this article are arranged in order of the degree for which they were submitted and then alphabetically by author. All items are listed, except for BA (hons.) dissertations in history, and are available in the University of Malta library.

587　**A bibliography of Maltese bibliographies.**
　　Paul Xuereb.　Msida, Valletta: University of Malta Library, 1978. 18p.
This work contains details of 121 bibliographies on Malta. There are brief notes on several of the items to indicate their scope, value or limitation. It also includes some Maltese and foreign unpublished dissertations, which are not normally covered in works of this kind.

588　**Conference on the acquisition and bibliography of Commonwealth and Third World literatures in English, October 1983. The Bibliograhical control and acquisition of Maltese books with special reference to literary works in the English language.**
　　Paul Xuereb.　London: Commonwealth Institute, Working Party on Library Holdings of Commonwealth Literature, 1983. p. 273-82. (Tabled Paper no. 5.)
A well-researched study which covers Maltese literature.

Index

The index is a single alphabetical sequence of authors (personal and corporate), titles of publications and subjects. Index entries refer both to main items and to other works mentioned in the notes to each item. Title entries are in italics. Numeration refers to the items as numbered.

A

A to Z of Malta and Gozo. Street and footpath guide of the Maltese islands 56
Abela, G. F 95, 161
  life and career 161
Abela, M. 370
Acculturation
  periodicals 567
Adami, Fenech 307
Adami, G. Z. 178
Adelaide, Queen
  visit to malta 186
Administration
  French rule 170
  Gozo 182
  law 323
  police force 324, 330
Afforestation 577
Africans 128
Agius, A. J. 108
Agreement between the Government of the United Kingdom and the Government of Malta with respect to the use of Military Facilities in Malta . . . 351
Agreement on Mutual Defence and Assistance between the Government of the United Kingdom of Great Britain and

Northern Ireland and the Government of Malta . . . 352
Agricultural Advisory Services 420
Agricultural development 373, 385, 415, 577
Agriculture 13, 20, 35, 115, 386
  afforestation 577
  agricultural leases 319
  animal husbandry 572
  bedrock 421
  bibliographies 577
  climate 425, 577
  cooperatives 420, 422, 577
  crop production 577
  dairy industry 577
  education 577
  expropriation of agricultural land 422
  farming equipment 422
  fruit trees 421
  geological conditions 421
  government subsidies 420, 422
  Gozo 423, 497
  horticulture 577
  hydrology 577
  impact on emigration patterns 422
  irrigation 421
  land tenure 422
  legislation 577
  living standards of farmers 420
  marketing 420, 422-423

Borg, M. A. 493
Borg Olivier, B. C. 157
Botany 95, 98
Bowen-Jones, H. 373
Bowerman, H. G. 339
Boz 497
Bradford, E. 148, 154, 191, 213, 280, 500
Bradley, R. N. 110
Branigan, J. J. 34
Brass Dolphins 15
Braun, H. 111, 494
Brazil
    Maltese emigrants 252
Brea, L. B. 112
Brennan, P. 193
Brief historical notes on some smaller churches in Valletta 289
Brincat, E. 194
Britain *see also* British rule
    agreement with Malta on mutual defence and assistance 352-353
    capture of Malta 178-179
    company law 332
    emigration of British nationals 14
    financial aid to Malta 353
    literary influence 488
    membership of EEC 354
    military bases 12, 19, 315, 346
    official publications on Malta-bibliography 581
    policy towards Mediterranean 144, 346-347
    relations with Malta 19, 351-354, 367, 369
    relations with USSR 211
    taxation 14
    universities 443
Britain in Malta 183
Britain in the Mediterranean and the defence of her naval stations 346
Britain's crown jewels: Malta 136
British Broadcasting Corporation – BBC 27
British Five Year Plan for Malta 404
British Malta, vol. 1, 1800-1872 178
British rule 19, 40, 136, 172, 175-186, 302-304, 306, 309, 315
    Church state relations 183
    constitutional reform 183, 321, 347, 353
    education 183

Italian influence 183
    legislation 175
    numismatics 539, 541-542
    postal service 439
British Survey, June 1960. Malta: on historical survey 137
Broadcasting 449
Broadley, A. M. 168
Brockman, E. 5-6
Bronze Age 108, 112, 118, 134
Bruce, M. W. 35
Brucellosis 443
Bryans, R. 7
Brydone, P. 46
Bugeja, P. 265
Buhagiar, H. 495
Building of Malta during the period of the Knights of St. John of Jerusalem 1530-1795 529
Bulletin 551
Bulletin of the Sovereign Order of Saint John of Jerusalem – Knights Hospitallers of Malta 214
Buontempo, A. 469
Burridge, W. 113
Buskett
    flora 106
    natural history 92
Buskett and its natural history 92
Busuttil, E. D. 272, 511
Butcher, M. 474
Butler, L. 215
Butterflies 105
Butterflies of the Maltese islands 105
Buttigieg, A. 470-471
Buttigieg, J. 546
Buxton, L. H. Dudley 36
Byron, Lord George Gordon 46

C

Calepino, A. 272
Calleja, G. 496
Calnan, D. J. 152, 216
Camera, pictures of Malta 30
Cameron, C.
    appointed Civil Commissioner for Malta 175
Camilleri, J. 518
Campbell, Dykes 48
Carapecchia, R. 536

Caravaggio, Michelangelo da 274,
502-503
Cardinals 290
Carnivals 174
Cart tracks 115-116, 118, 130
Carthage
cultural connections with Malta 36
Cartography
16th century 37
Cartoons 504
Caruana, A. A. 114
Caruana Galijia, A. 508
Caruana Galijia, H. 508
Caruana Gatto, A. 91
Caruana, M. (Lino) 57
Cass, Z. 472
Cassar, G. N. 405
Cassar, P. 115, 355, 443-445
Cassar Pullicino, J. 512-514
Cassola, G. 484
Castello
travel guides 53
Castles 165, 342
Catacombs 115
Catalano-Aragonese power in the
Mediterranean
influence of Malta 150
*Catalogue of the Foster Stearns
Collection on the Sovereign
Military Order of St. John of
Jerusalem, called, of Malta* 231
*Catalogue of the records of the Order
of St. John of Jerusalem in the
Royal Malta Library* 235
Cathedral Museum 80
Cathedral of Mdina 526
Catholic Church 7, 12, 19, 27, 257
abolition of ecclesiastical immunities
276
and politics 275, 286, 295-296, 303
and social change 298
archbishops 287
as focus of national identity 298
bishops 291, 300
cardinals 290
clergy concubinage 28
conflict with Labour party 295-296,
307, 315
creation of diocese of Gozo 277
cult of saints 275
Franciscans 282
Hal-Farrug 4

history 113, 125, 141, 147, 178,
276-278, 280-284, 286, 290-291,
293, 297-300
immunity of priests from secular
courts (19th century) 49
in USA 237
Inquisition 166
John the Baptist 283-284
Knights of St. John 213
links with nobility 163
Maltese Episcopal Conference 276
newspapers 556
relationship between regular and
secular clergy 294
role in the community 27
role of the Knights of St. John 237
rural areas 275
St. Paul 7, 113, 125, 280, 299
structural differentiation 298
Vatican 286
Catholic life in Malta AD60-1960 281
Cauchi, J. 492
Cauchi, R. 58
Cavaliero, R. 217
Caves 115
Census of the Maltese Islands 431
Censuses 36, 253, 431
Central Bank of Malta 399
*Central Bank of Malta Act, 1967 and
subsequent amendments 1983* 399
*Central Bank of Malta: Quarterly
Review, December 1984* 400
Centuries look down 111
Century of progress, 1848-1948 374
*Certified opinion on the possibilities of
a development of tourism in Malta*
417
Chamber of Commerce 374, 401, 406
*Charisma of the primitive Franciscan
fraternity* 282
Charles V, Holy Roman Emperor 232
*Checklist of Maltese periodicals and
newspapers in the National Library
of Malta (formerly Royal Malta
Library) and University of Malta
Library* 579
Chesney, A. G. 340
Chetcuti, G. 473
Cholera 443
Christian Workers Party 326
view of draft constitution (1963) 326
Chronologies 26

colloquial 267
development 259-260, 266, 269
dialect 263
dictionaries 271-273
English loanwords 262
grammar 270
idioms 263
Italian 269, 286
Italian loanwords 262
journalistic 267
lexicography 261
linguistics 260-263
literary 267
Maltese alphabet 26
nicknames 263
orthography 261
Persian 269
Phoenician influence 262
phonetic change 261
phonology 262
proverbs 263, 271
relationship with culture 259
relationship with politics 259
Romance languages 261
semantics 261
Semitic languages 261
spelling 6, 266
spoken 267
surnames 263
teaching 266, 268
toponymy 1, 261, 263
vocabulary 270
Laspina, S. 140
*Last bastion, sketches of the Maltese
islands* 6
*Last of the crusaders: the Knights of St.
John in Malta in the 18th century*
217
Laucht, I. 408
Law and the legal system 318
agricultural leases 319
autobiographies 332
banking 335
commercial partnerships 320
Commercial Partnerships Ordinance
334
company law 333
governmental liability 323
human rights 322
judges 318, 330
Metayer System 319
penal system 449

periodicals 568
police force 324, 330
*Law on commercial partnerships in
Malta* 320
Lawrence, D. H. 46
Leap of Malta dolphins 478
Lear, Edward 46-47
Leaver, A. J. 360
Lee, H. I. 347
Legends, Norman 151
Legislation
agriculture 577
labour relations 427
Lehen is-Sewwa 558
Leisure activities 6
diving 547
gardening 546, 549
rock climbing 548
swimming 7
Leitch, V. 99
Leopardi, E. P. 162
Leopardi, E. R. 532
Lepidoptera 105, 107
Leprosy 443, 448
Levant 165
trade with the Dutch 540
Lewis, H. 64, 122
Lewis, V. 484
Libraries
Malta University 578-579, 585-586
National Library of Malta 579,
583
Libya
relations with Malta 356, 365
Licari, J. 403
Liebers, A. 100
Liebich, F. K. 408
Lieutenant governors
Ponsonby 175
Life and customs 5-7, 9, 11, 17-18, 21,
24-25, 27-28, 31, 84, 139,
511-512, 514
Gozo 471
Hal-Farrug 4
history 173-174
Mediterranean region 24
periodicals 517
tradition 16, 139
*Life and times of Vicenzo Labini,
Bishop of Malta* 291
Linguistics 260-263
history 141

147

Megalithic art 127
Megalithic art of the Maltese islands 127
Megalithic monuments 119
  use of spiral pattern 119
Megalithic monuments of Malta 119
Megalithic peoples 119
  astronomy 119
  mathematics 119
  monuments 119
  mysticism 119
Melita Historica 142, 520
Melitensia: Books in Print 575
Melitensia: a catalogue of printed books and articles in the Royal University of Malta Library referring to Malta 585
Melitensia 1900-1975. Catalogue of the Exhibition held at St. John's Annexe, Valletta, June 3-15, 1975 141
Mellieha Bay
  mortar wreck 120
  travel guides 87
Mercieca, A. 332
Mesolithic Age 112
Metayer System 319
Metwally, M. M. 378, 390
Mġarr 133
  social conditions 422
Micallef, H. 93
Micallef, J. 203, 333, 362
Micallef, R. E. 446
Michelangelo Merisi da Caravaggio 503
Midwifery 443-444
Migration
  Eurafricans and Mediterranean races 110
  treaties 361
Military
  links with USSR 359
  treaties 361
Military bases 160
  British 12, 19, 315, 346, 351
  economic importance 315, 351, 369-370
  Knights of St. John 160
Military history 142, 345
  British capture of Valletta 349
  castles 342
  civil defence 338
  fortifications 2, 117, 216
  Knights of St. John 213, 248

  navy 341
  Regiment of Militia 340
  Royal Malta Artillery 340, 344, 350
  Royal Oak courts martial 343
  sea power 348
Miller, P. 484
Ministry of Trade 407
Milne, R. G. 391
Minorities
  Jews 258
Mintoff, Dom 295, 306-307, 326, 356, 392, 395, 404
  early political and economic views 392
  economic policy 388
  foreign policy 357, 362, 367
  statement at Independence Conference 326
Mizzi, Dr. E. F. 158
Mizzi, F. P. 310
Mizzi, J. 235
Mizzi, L. F. 269
Modern Movement in architecture
  impact on Richard England 531
Mojana, Fra' A. de 236
  visit to Malta 236
Mollicone, A. 534
Mompalo de Piro, J. C. 549
Monopolies 415
Monsarrat, N. 486
Montalto, J. 163
Monuments and memorials 173
  Great Siege Monument 173
Monuments of Mdina – the ancient capital city of Malta and its art treasures 80
More, J. 24
Moroso, N. 237
Morris, T. O. 437
Mortar wreck in Mellieha Bay, plans and soundings. A report on the 1967 campaign carried out on behalf of the National Museum of Malta 120
Moslems 148-149
Mosta Rotunda
  guide 58
  history 58
Mosta Rotunda, short history and guide 58
Moths 107
  Gozo 107

Roman Catholic Church *cont.*
structural differentiation 298
Vatican 286
Roman period 122
economy 28
Roman villa 526
Roman villa in history 537
Roman villas
Mdina 537
Rabat 537
Romance languages
links with Maltese 261
Romano Carrapecchia: studies in Maltese architecture I 536
Rome 229, 286
cultural connections with Malta 36
Rommel, Erwin 206
Ronzitti, N. 368
Roosevelt, Franklin D. 211
Rose, H. 77
Rose, J. Holland 176
Roskill, O. W. 415
Roth, C. 258
Round Table Conference 306, 329, 331
Royal Air Force
torpedo bombers 188
World War II 188
Royal Anthropological Institute 27
Royal Commission (1877)
account of Maltese nobility 250
Royal Malta Artillery
history 340, 344, 350
Royal Malta Library *see also* Malta Library
manuscript holdings 117
Royal Navy 209, 339
Mediterranean policy in World War II 209
'Royal Oak' courts martial 343
Royal Oak (vessel) 343
Royal Opera House, Malta 493
bombing 506
engravings depicting its foundation 504
fire 506
fire – portrayal in novel 482
Royal University of Malta *see also* Malta University 121, 172, 422
theses and dissertations 586
Royal University of Malta Library 585-586
newspaper holdings 579

periodical holdings 578-579
Royal University of Malta Library Melitensia Collection. List of periodical holdings 578
Royal visit to Malta, November, 1967 314
Royal visits
British Royal Family (1967) 314
engravings 504
Queen Victoria 173-174
Russian Empress 177
Royle, P. Y. 92, 106
Rural areas
religion and politics 275
Russia 283
Russia, Empress of
visit to Malta 177
Ruston, M. 473

S

Sacks, H. R. 78
Sacred art 492
Sacred art in Malta 492
Sacred Infirmary 226
Said, E. 544
Said Malta Coin, Banknote and Medal Catalogue, 1982 544
St. Barbara, Church of 289, 536
St. Catherine, Church of 289, 536
St. James, Church of 289, 536
St. John's Annexe
historical exhibition (1975) 141
St. John's Cathedral 81, 274, 297, 503
St. John's Gate 239
St. John's Gate: headquarters of the Order of St. John 239
St. Lucia, Church of 289
St. Luke 278
St. Paul 7
shipwreck on Malta 113, 125, 299
stay on Malta 125, 280, 299, 439
St. Paul, Christ's envoy to Malta: AD60-1960 299
St. Paul's Square 80
St. Roque, Church of 289
St. Scholastica Convent 220
Saints 7
Saints and fireworks: religion and politics in rural Malta 275
Salvatore, Father

Map of Malta

This map shows the more important towns and other features.